Writing Worlds 1
The Norwich Exchanges
Edited by Vesna Goldsworthy

New Writing Worlds is an annual series of international dialogues and literary projects that brings together writers from around the world to celebrate the act of writing and debate the nature of literature across cultures. At the heart of the programme is a symposium held at the world-renowned centre for creative writing, the University of East Anglia, and a series of public events, readings and workshops. The New Writing Worlds series was launched in 2005, when 40 writers from around the globe came to Norwich to discuss the concept of 'Literary Value.' Each year's events will be informed by a different thematic starting point, and culminate in a final international congress in 2009 to which all former participants will be invited.

The series is organized by The New Writing Partnership in collaboration with The University of East Anglia and is being supported by Arts Council England, East, The City of Norwich and The County of Norfolk. Writing Worlds 2: The Norwich Exchanges will be published in 2006.

Writing Worlds 1: The Norwich Exchanges is a joint venture between The New Writing Partnership and Pen & Inc Press at the University of East Anglia.

The New Writing Partnership is a newly established literary organization in the East of England committed to promoting and encouraging outstanding talent in creative writing and to fostering international debate around contemporary literature. It is supported by the University of East Anglia, Norwich City Council, Norfolk County Council, and Arts Council England, East.

The New Writing Partnership

UEA NORWICH

ARTS COUNCIL ENGLAND

NORWICH City Council

Norfolk County Council

Thanks to the following for making Pen & Inc Press possible: the School of Literature and Creative Writing, the Centre for Creative and Performing Arts, Professor Jon Cook and Val Striker at the University of East Anglia.

Pen & Inc Press

Managing Editor: Katri Skala
General Manager: Sarah Gooderson
Design and Production: Emma Forsberg

The New Writing Partnership

Director: Trevor Davies
Programme Director for New Writing Worlds: Katri Skala
Symposium Director: Jon Cook
Office Manager: Leila Telford
Programme Researcher and Co-ordinator: Jude Piesse

Writing Worlds 1: The Norwich Exchanges is published by Pen & Inc Press (2006), School of Literature and Creative Writing, University of East Anglia, Norwich, Norfolk, NR4 7TJ

Introduction © Jon Cook, 2006
Selection and Afterword © Vesna Goldsworthy, 2006
International © retained by individual authors, 2006

A CIP record for this book is available from the British Library

ISBN: 1-902913-26-4

Writing Worlds 1 is distributed by Central Books, 99 Wallace Road, London, E9 5LN. Pen & Inc Press is a member of Inpress Ltd. – Independent Presses Management. Printed and bound by Antony Rowe Ltd., Bumper's Farm, Chippenham, Wiltshire SN14 6LH.

Contents

Writing and Moral Duty

Writing, Language, Translation

Writing Futures

This book is partly a record and mostly a transformation of an event. The nature of this event is not easy to summarize or describe. It took place in a city, Norwich, and at a university, the University of East Anglia, in June 2005. It was a gathering of writers from many different parts of the world. Some of the time was spent in readings and discussions held in the Forum building in the centre of Norwich. So the event was like a literary festival, bringing readers to hear the work of writers, often writers with international reputations but curiously unheard of in this country. The event was like a writers' workshop, too. People who had never deliberately written a fiction in their lives before were invited to do so, as were others who had some experience of creative writing.

In addition to these two aspects – the literary festival, the writing workshop – there was a third, a symposium on the topic of literary value. This was an occasion where the writers invited to attend had no other immediate audience but themselves. The discussion that ensued is the subject of this book.

Such a discussion might seem doubtful from the start. 'Literary value' has a forbidding ring to it. It is dogmatically singular and summons the idea of people who know what they like, and worse still, want to insist that you should like it too. Perhaps it's better to be confused about the topic, or confidently sceptical. I may like a novel or a poem but that's not a reason for anybody else to like them. Literary pleasures are private, bedtime things, or, if they're shared enthusiasms, they're no more than that. The increase in numbers makes no qualitative difference. It's a fortunate coincidence if other people happen to like what I like to read. Shared tastes cannot be imposed on people who don't share them. You can't decide for others what they will like.

This diffidence about literary value is reinforced by a scepticism that argues there's no such thing in the first place. The basic argument is clear and, I imagine, familiar: judgments of literary value are contaminated by interests, whether of class, gender, or ethnicity, or some mixture of all of these. A literary culture gives systematic order to these interests through its power to include and exclude what will count as literature. When I say I like a book what I'm in fact doing – probably unconsciously, but maybe not – is promoting a power that benefits me.

We live in a world of 'cultural constructs'. The agent and the entrepreneur of these constructions is power not justice. Within this world there can be a kind of literary value for works of imagination that oppose a dominant power and give voice to the silenced. But the value we give to these works as literature is heavily dependent upon a political value and commitment. In this context, literary value can't survive on its own. It has no claim on us in its own right.

The diffident voice and the sceptical voice seem to have a settled presence in discussions about literary value. If we add to them a third – the voice of the market – then further discussion seems pointless. Here the position is equally clear. What sells is what's good. The market mechanism may be a bit clumsy at times – it once overlooked Joyce's *Ulysses*, for example, and countless other works – but it's the best way we have of making decisions about literary value. There's a kind of democracy here, after all. What lots of people buy – Dan Brown's *The Da Vinci Code* is the current example – is what's good. Value is success in the market. Take it or leave it.

These three voices, in their contradictory chorus, compose a desolate scene. But they're by no means all there is. The last decade in Britain has seen the emergence of different kinds of readers' groups. What they share in common is a desire to discuss, among people who are not 'literary specialists', how a book works and whether it's good. The question of literary value might still be worth raising. It might be that there was not just something more to be said on the subject but something that needed to be said. It was important, too, that a group of writers should be involved in the saying, and that it should be an international group. The process of writing is an endless negotiation with the question of value, not necessarily as some ultimate end or goal, but as a matter of practice. The sense of whether a sentence or line should be included or not, the decision to complete a chapter, a stanza, a poem or a book at a certain point – all these and a multitude of other decisions and impulses depend, however tacitly, on a sense of value, on what is going to bring a work to its best state of realization, or to the best available at the time. Bringing this experience to bear – the experience of writers as readers of their own and others' work – seemed to be a good place to renew the debate.

Jon Cook 7

It might seem an obvious place to start. In the early 20th century, Ezra Pound had insisted that no attention should be paid 'to the criticism of men who have never themselves written a notable work'. It seemed obvious to him that literary achievement was a better qualification for thinking about literary value than knowledge of a critical theory. Yet by the early 21st century this view had come to seem out of date. A pronounced division of labour had taken hold, especially in the academy. 'Literary value' has become a subject for specialists, and writers, with all their anxieties abut reputation and their immersion in the world of practice, are the last persons to look to for guidance on the topic. What had been taken for granted in the first half of the 20th century – that good poets, novelists and dramatists could be, and often were, notable critics – had lost its purchase. The 'creative writer' and the 'critic/theorist' have become polarized figures. It's part of this new mythology, of course, that the one group, the critic/theorists, had pronounced the death of the second, the authors.

This mythology, always superficial and misleading, seems to have lost any of the intellectual vitality and challenge it might once have had. The idea informing the symposium, that writers might be consulted about the question of literary value, was not intended as a nostalgic gesture. If a past was evoked at all, it was only to challenge the complacencies of the present, and to hold out the possibility of a new connection between writing literature and thinking about it critically.

It seemed self-evident that any productive conversation about literary value would have to take place between writers from different nations and from none. Literature travels more rapidly from one country to another than ever before. The rise of English as a global language raises acute questions about the survival of literatures in minority languages. We live in the midst of a sophisticated international literary economy that allows some works to travel first class while others scarcely get on the plane. 'Globalization' has paradoxical effects. We might think that it allows work produced in one country or place to be read in another. But often this is not the case. Britain, in this respect, may be an odd case or it may be typical. What is certainly true is that work of great distinction, written by authors existing outside or on the margins of the Anglo-American literary economy, scarcely finds a readership here. There is a constant danger that 'globalization' will simply produce new provincialisms of literary experience. The cosmopolitan character of the group of writers who contributed to the symposium was intended to open up an understanding of just how much was going on outside the customary boundaries of what passes for internationalism in Britain.

***

The organization of this first Writing Worlds book corresponds to the sequence of sessions that made up the symposium. Each of the sessions was initiated or sustained by short 20-minute statements from some of the writers who attended. These form the basis for the longer pieces that are threaded through the book. In between are edited transcripts of some of the discussions that took place in each session. This forms the basis for the first five sections of the book. In addition there is a brief section that discusses readers, and then some personal statements about what for an individual writer composes his or her writing world. Finally, the book's editor, Vesna Goldsworthy, provides an afterword that reflects on her experience of the Norwich conversations.

Each of the book's sections provides an orientation and starting point for thinking about the question of literary value. How does literature become valuable when we think about it in relation to the past, or to place, or to ethical concerns, or to the issue of translation, or to the future? The arguments move through different dimensions of personal, historical and political experience and understanding. Each section contains articulate and committed statements about what makes literature valuable. They also contain questions, debate, controversy and admissions of loss. The book's form, and the editorial skill that has gone into its making, raise an important question about how we might think about literary value. Perhaps the different orientations turn literary value from a singular into a plural. Does this movement from the singular to the plural, from value to values, mean that we can only think about the question by way of fragments? Or is it possible to think in the singular and the plural at the same time, to move from one perspective to another and discover some resemblance between them, a common thread that runs through these conversations and controversies?

Jon Cook 9

It is not the purpose of this book to provide answers to these questions, but it does provide material both clear enough and critical enough to think further about them. You will not find a good student's answer here to the primly posed question 'what is literary value?' What you will find is a diversity of experience, commitment and critical passion that makes the question worth asking in the first place.

Writing Worlds 1
The Norwich Exchanges

Writing and the Past

The past is one of the basic materials and foodstuffs of writing. Its uses are as multiple and attitudes to it as variable as the writerly sensibilities that are brought to bear upon it. So I can only make a rather arbitrary foray into this enormous territory, and propose some categories or ways of thinking about the past that happen to be meaningful to me, and that I hope are more broadly suggestive as well. Let me say at the outset that I am going to talk not mainly about the question of literary traditions, but about various relationships to the past and memory, as these infuse imaginative writing.

My own writing emerged initially from the experience of emigration and exile, a condition which many of you in this room are familiar with, and which tremendously magnifies and foregrounds the problems of the past and its meanings. The rupture of exile encourages an internal rupture as well – a rift in which the past is all of a sudden on one side of the divide, the present on the other. From this vantage point, certain things which might otherwise be taken for granted become both problematic and very evident. For me, even though I was a very young immigrant, being ejected from my first world – and particularly from my first language – held some very quick lessons about not only my immediate, but also the longer past. Of course, what I missed initially were friends, teachers, the countryside, the beautiful urban landscape of Krakow. But over and above that, what that first period of dislocation made evident was the importance of certain more impalpable entities which I would not have noticed or understood had I not been uprooted; and by these, I mean the large and seemingly abstract entities of language and culture. Being, for a while, in effect without language made me realize that it is not only something that we use or even communicate with; rather, it is something that lives within us, which deeply shapes or even creates our internal lives. To be without language is to risk having no ways of articulating or perceiving the world; indeed, it risks a loss of a subjective, inner life.

As with language, so with culture. What emigration made evident to me is how much we are creatures of culture, how much confusion and loss of self we risk when we fall out of its matrix. By culture, I mean not only the articulated traditions of literature, art, political ideologies or history (important though all of these are), but also the symbolic meanings and attitudes that shape our mental world, our orientation towards others, our sense of what it is to be a person, a man or a woman. That kind of culture, which comes from accumulated layers of the past, is transmitted to us from our earliest days through the family and our first intimates, through gestures and everyday commentary, through the rhythms of language and what might be called the 'music of selfhood'. Literature, of course, eventually comes to be an important part of this larger matrix; but if I dwell on these broader and less tangible strata of transmission, it is because this is a meaning of the past which I think is sometimes forgotten. We tend to think about the past as something outside us, some enormous storehouse or coffer, in which we can rummage, and which is filled with either fabulous gifts and treasures or horrid and unsightly items that we'd prefer to discard and disown. But there is also a past that wends itself across generations, from psyche to psyche, and which is so deeply internalized that we don't so much remember it as carry it or embody it within us. This is of course a past which inevitably informs whatever we may write. It's the compelling force of one's first heritage that it is embedded and embodied so deeply as to be an intrinsic part of ourselves and our perceptions.

What happens when you are severed from the primary and, so to speak, deep past? Such a rupture, aside from foregrounding the past itself, highlights certain attitudes towards the past, and also their possible excesses and dangers.

Nostalgia, I think, is the first temptation of exile. For those of us who have experienced this condition, it may be the present for a while which is another country and the past which is the familiar and the longed-for home. Joyce Carol Oates has said in a striking formulation that 'for most novelists the art of writing might be defined as the use to which we put our homesickness. The instinct to memorialize one's region, one's family, one's past is so strong that without it many writers would be rendered paralysed and mute.' In exile, the impulse to memorialize is magnified and much wonderful literature has emerged from it. Nostalgia can be a very lyrical emotion. The danger, to my mind, of such a preoccupation with the past, of a too insistent backwards gaze, is that lyrical nostalgia can turn into melancholic mourning. The past becomes idealized into a sort of unchangeable, frozen pastoral.

This is one of the perils of exile, in the sense that you don't have a chance to revise the past in a natural way. You don't have a chance to go back to the home in which you grew up and see that, actually, it is smaller and less enfolding than remembered, or to go back into your old neighbourhood and notice the conflicts and tensions that you didn't sense as a child. In other words, when you are severed from the past, you don't have a chance to perform natural revisions on it, and so the past can become immobilized at the point at which you left it. One's attitude towards it is in danger of becoming quite fixed and rigid. On a collective level, the duty to remember, an obsessive loyalty, can turn into a sort of arrested nationalism, for example, or other rigid ideologies. Arrested, because the nationalism of exiles usually refers to the country they left behind, rather than to new or changing realities. In literature, such attitudes can become manifested through excessive sentimentality about lost homes and homelands, or in a classicizing cast of mind, which places all the glories in some classical age, and thinks that all we can do is produce diminished or imitative versions of former greatness.

At the opposite end of the spectrum from nostalgia is the tendency to reject or even demonize the past, to view it as nothing but an oppression or a prison or, in any case, as inferior to whatever new world into which one has come. Such a tendency was encouraged, for example in the America that I came to, and the assimilationist ethos which prevailed through the 1960s and the 1970s. The idea of the 'melting pot' was that new immigrants should become American immediately and without regret. Forget those quaint old worlds, this ideology enjoined, and get with the programme. Many new immigrants agreed and tried eagerly to 'put the past behind them,' as the saying goes, and join with the forces of the future and progress. To be personal for a moment, the reason I couldn't accomplish this leap as easily as I was supposed to was because I felt that this kind of instant forgetfulness and rejection of the past would leave me not only without strata of self, but also without instruments with which to perceive the new world and start understanding its traditions and vernacular. What I wanted to do was to transport the intensity of the first attachments and relationships to the past over to this new culture. Above all, I wanted English – my new language – to inhabit me quite fully and really to live within my psyche, rather than just serve as something I could use, or of which I had more or less a command.

Eva Hoffman 15

For obvious reasons, this 'rejectionist' tendency is found less frequently in literature. Unlike nostalgia, the urge to forget, or amnesia, is not good fuel for writing. But perhaps in general terms, one can discern this set of attitudes in a kind of overreaching scepticism or a desire to deconstruct all given meanings, that marks a certain kind of literature. Or perhaps we can discern this attitude in writing that prefers to sing the glories of here and now; or in a modernist cast of mind, within which we who live now are always more progressive than anything that has come before, and which enjoins us to overthrow all conventions and 'make it new' from ground zero, as if nothing worthwhile or interesting had gone on before us.

I suppose one needs to insert a realist perspective here: it is easier to try to reject or forget a past that was unhappy or harsh. If your personal history included a spell in the Soviet Gulag, you are not likely to remember it fondly. But even so, denial does not seem to be a salutary or literarily rich response. I think a severance from the past can be painful, even if the past itself was painful. For me, this realization came as I was writing about the effects of a transmitted past – in this case, the legacy of war and the Holocaust. This is the most sombre kind of past imaginable. And yet, I realized that for many survivors who emigrated far from the sites of their suffering and losses, part of the hardship that followed was finding themselves in places where their very dark history was not understood or had no significance. This created a kind of isolation that increased the burden of remembering. A difficult history shared is a history made more bearable. Indeed, perhaps one of the great uses of writing about the past is that it helps us to think about our histories in common, and that it creates those imagined communities which Benedict Anderson talks about.

As it happens, I come from two cultures – Polish and Jewish – that both have long traditions of exilic literature. Both experienced long periods in various kinds of diaspora. And both survived to a large extent by books, by recording and preserving collective memories through writing. As we look upon the 20th century we see that much of its literature came out of the rupture of exile and the perspectives on the past that it creates. Nabokov's *Speak, Memory*, or Brodsky's essays, or the poems of Czeslaw Milosz, or even Milan Kundera's much cooler take on transplantation, are all works of commemoration and reflection on the past. These works are often informed by a tenderness for what seems to be lost, but also by the need, or even the obligation, to remember. An obligation because these writers, and so many others from different parts of the world, were talking about suppressed and censored histories. And this, too, is one of the strong uses of literature, especially in marginal or suppressed cultures: to bear witness and give voice to unofficial histories, to aspects of the past that might otherwise be forgotten or wilfully distorted or denied. In that sense, writing not only uses the past but participates in its creation, and in the shaping of collective memories.

All of these writers and many others have drawn upon the richest potential of the exilic perspective – for in the best case scenario, being 'in-between' can provide a vantage point both on what is left behind and the new worlds we enter. It can leave you with the perceptual mobility, so to speak, to revise and reinterpret both the past and the present. The great enlargement of a transcultural journey is that it can eventually allow you to enter fully into the subjectivity and internal life of another culture, with its store of memories, traditions and literary vocabularies. For we can, of course, make use of more than one tradition and bring them into fruitful interplay. I think, for example, of the work of Czeslaw Milosz, which is marked by a very strong impulse to witness and remember – to witness especially the period of the Second World War, and to remember in the service of truth, because much of the history he lived through was later so wilfully denied and distorted. But he also brought his capacious curiosity to bear on American literature and culture and, more profoundly, he used exile as an occasion for a kind of metaphysical wonderment about the different dimensions of time and reality in which he lived.

In all of these observations, I've been making an implicit distinction between the kind of past that is deeply internalized, and what might be called the external past of more distant history – the history we learn about or from, but which does not initially carry a cargo of psychic weight and meanings. In other words, I suppose I have been making a distinction between memory – including memory transmitted across generations – and history. After a century of psychoanalytic thinking about memory, we could almost make a sort of catalogue of its various distortions and misuses: hysterical displacement, obsessive fixation, repression, etc. But I have also found very helpful the psychoanalytic notion that it is only when we arrive at a full remembering – the kind of remembering that happens through a process of reflection and musing, and maybe of writing – that the past can cease its haunting, and become separate from the present; and that it is only then that both the past and the present can be seen in their own light. Perhaps the richest use of the past in writing is for the creation of a kind of interplay, a dialectic in which both the past and the present can illuminate each other. We can, especially through the process of imaginative writing, revise and reconstruct, playfully and/or seriously. And we can also think about the very constructions of memory, which, as George Szirtes said, are a kind of necessary fiction (but a fiction, nevertheless), which has its own illuminating truthfulness.

The pleasures of writing about the external past can of course be considerable: they are the pleasures of exploration and discovery, and of viewing the world from a kind of brisk and clarifying distance. In fiction, I suppose, that kind of relationship to the past is likely to result in the historical novel, with all its bracing possibilities. But I think it is the internalized past that is the specific and special domain of imaginative writing. I have not yet read the much-debated book by John Carey, *What Good Are The Arts?*, but although I suspect I would disagree with many of its conclusions, the questions it poses are ones we need to think about. In a mass culture and society, what is the value of the arts? What good is literature? What are its particular purposes?

For me at least, a large part of the answer lies in the capacity of imaginative writing to paint and delineate internal landscapes, with their very specific narratives, valences of experience and textures of memory. More than works of scholarship or political commentary or moral philosophy even, literature can give us glimpses of the subjective worlds of others; it can show us not what it is to be a good or better person, but what it is to be a person with a particular subjectivity, living through a particular set of circumstances, pasts and histories. In that sense, and insofar as imaginative writing allows us access to experiences and pasts of others as well as our own, it seems to me to be a very necessary and powerful instrument of understanding, and certainly a very important part of our common cultural and cross-cultural conversations.

18 Writing and the Past

Languages of Exile: Tradition and Literary Value

In conversation: Gillian Beer, Ron Butlin, Jon Cook, Alison Croggon, Vesna Goldsworthy, Eva Hoffman, Ogaga Ifowodo, Kapka Kassabova, Tessa de Loo, David Solway, George Szirtes, Luisa Valenzuela and Mary Woronov

David Solway:

Both in her essay presented here and in her wonderful memoir, *Lost in Translation*, Eva Hoffman brings up so many different issues with such complexity, on so many different levels, that my immediate reaction is vertigo and where-to-go.

The first question I'd like to ask Eva is: how do you regard the notion, the condition, the problem of exile, when it applies to somebody who is not, from the traditional perspective, in a condition of exile? I believe exile is a condition, like a virus, that we all carry within us. Some of us suffer from it more grievously than others, especially when we have been displaced, as you have. But what about those who have not been displaced? Are they in some sense also under the hammer of exile? Is there a kind of diaspora, a kind of displacement, which actually pertains to people who do not visibly suffer from the disorientation that you have experienced?

As a Jew growing up in a French-Canadian town in Quebec, I have experienced a certain notion of exile, and I carry it with me in this chipped tooth and the sling shot that left this cleft right here, a cleft which is not a result of deep cogitation. I wonder about those people who attacked me for being a Jew, for being different, and for speaking in a different accent. Those people seemed so much at home in what was, at that time, the Catholic Church.

What kind of exile did these people experience? I never formulated that question when I was a child in that particular way; I would say: are they unhappy too? And in what way are they unhappy? They didn't seem unhappy compared to the kind of unhappiness I felt. It was only later on that I realized that they too were experiencing something that was a modification of what I was going through, certainly what Eva has gone through. How would we describe a concept of exile which applies to those who are very much at home?

Eva Hoffman:

I think that the sensation of being at home is actually much harder to attain than the sensation of being on the margins, in exile. We all stand at various angles to mainstream culture, communities, traditions or even our selves. In a sense, I was using exile as a metaphor for certain kinds of movement from the past into the present. It does strike me that the sense of being at home is something that we haven't decoded as much as we have a sense of being in exile.

Gillian Beer:

When I read *Lost in Translation* I was struck that the condition you describe is also the condition of leaving childhood. In that sense we all have had the experience of exile. Our bodies have changed so utterly; those fragments that we recall from our past, from our childhood, happened to a little being who is not and yet is us. I feel that it is a very profound experience that we all share, whether or not we stayed at home.

Eva Hoffman:

One of the functions of a post-Freudian or a post-Romantic aftermath is that we are all in exile from a blissful or unblissful childhood. We all experience this passage into the other life.

George Szirtes:

There is a phrase you used: 'remembering how the past can become itself'. It is one of those mystical sorts of statements. In what ways do things become themselves? How do we recognize the past becoming itself? How do we recognize these truths?

Eva Hoffman:

You are right, it is a kind of idealized state that perhaps can never be fully achieved. I was thinking about how the past can impinge upon us, haunt us and overwhelm the present so that we cannot see the present in its own light. Again this is something that may be amplified by homesickness or emigration. Sometimes it is a function of having lived through a very difficult experience, a difficult history. I was thinking about it particularly when I was writing my last book, *After Such Knowledge*, which is about the legacy of the war and the Holocaust. The past can haunt us in very unconscious ways and can infect our understanding of the present as well.

I think we have all thought about it on a political level – uses of memory in the Yugoslav war, for example – distortions of memory and former defeats contributing to martial patriotic feelings in the present. I was simply thinking of making the unconscious conscious; a very old psychoanalytic formula of articulating and thinking about the past to the point where it can be seen as separate from the present, as something that you can have a view of.

Vesna Goldsworthy:

Eva, I was really interested in the connections between exile and language. You said at one point that you wanted to inhabit the English language. It is a desire that I share; the reason I chose to write in English. Do you think that there is a kind of quintessential difference in terms of nostalgia between such choices of language? Quite a lot of writers in exile are very protective about their desire to inhabit their land of origin by continuing to write in their mother tongue.

Eva Hoffman:

I think that circumstances do need to be taken into account. I was young enough when I emigrated to make the shift into English and, in a sense, absolutely had to make that shift, because Polish became a kind of unusable language. It had no place. It became my great project to transpose the relationship I had to Polish into English. There is a kind of circumstantial and cognitive aspect to it – it is simply more difficult to do it later in life.

Tessa de Loo:

Don't you think that the act of writing makes us outsiders? It is a kind of self-chosen exile, an exile from our society. That's one of the thoughts that came to me when you were talking about exile. I left my country 12 years ago because I didn't want to live there anymore. I chose my own exile. These two different kinds of exile – being a writer and being an outsider – they've melded through time.

Mary Woronov:

You said, being a writer, you feel exiled. I have a similar point – as I became a writer I realized I was born an outsider. In the act of writing I am able to sever the past from the present – it does not dominate me anymore. It's a healing thing. In truth, it's very human. As I wrote I realized what an outsider I was. If I did not write I doubt that I would have made that realization. I would have been locked into the past.

Alison Croggon:

My father was a mining engineer. He went to South Africa from England, then back. Then, when I was seven, he went to Australia and lived there. Listening to the discussion about language, I was thinking about the kinds of difference that happen when you assume that you can communicate because you speak the same language. Going from England to Australia undermined that assumption. I became very conscious of huge fractures and gaps in meaning. A tree didn't mean the same thing in England and Australia. It's not like the immediate, dramatic thing of losing a language but it was oddly similar. Poetry, in particular, for me, was a way of trying to mend this and integrate the past into the present.

Jon Cook:

We're talking about the centrality of this relationship between the past and the present, and seeing exile in some sense as both a fact of historical and personal existence, and a kind of metaphor for describing the relationship between the past and the present. What fascinates me about this is: in what sense is the practice of writing, perhaps especially of imaginative writing, of value here in a way that, for example, going to see an analyst, lying on the couch, engaging in the talking cure, is or isn't? I was very struck by what

Eva said, when she explained that moving away from her first language, Polish, into this new language, English, gave her a heightened sensuous apprehension of the new language. That new language came into a sort of palpable existence that it might not have had, had she been a native speaker. I'm reminded there of a very interesting remark made by the 18th-century philosopher Diderot who said that poets treat their own language as if it were a foreign language; they don't actually dwell in their own language as though it were their own. I think this raises some interesting questions about what it means to own a language. Do we ever own a language? What is it that writing does in this context?

David Solway:

As you were speaking I was thinking of Joseph Conrad who, as we all know, wrote and spoke Polish as his first language. French was effectively his second language, and he decided to write in his third, English. As a result of that he has become, as far as I'm concerned, one of the great and most influential writers of our time. Eva, as I was reading your book, which is so beautifully written that, I must say, my initial reaction to you was envy, I was wondering if you did not choose to write in English in the same sense that Conrad did. Let's say that you had not been displaced in the way that you were, and you were writing in Polish, not in English, I wonder if you've ever asked yourself that question reflexively – had you been a Polish writer, writing your memoirs in Polish – do you think you would have achieved the same degree of sensuous intellectualism that you have here, in this particular book?

Eva Hoffman:

Well, certainly having a language thrust upon you, which was my situation, heightens the awareness of language altogether. Had I written in Polish it would certainly have been a very different form of writing. I might not have had to be so self-conscious and reflect so much on the question of language itself. I can't think of many writers who have chosen to write in a different language. Beckett, of course, is one. He chose to do so precisely for the virtues of defamiliarization, of gaining a certain distance and therefore a certain consciousness of language. But as to all of us writing in a foreign language, I'm reminded of something that Auden said. Let me paraphrase: poetry emerges from an initial mistake that the child makes. The nanny points to the moon. The child thinks that the word moon is the moon. This is of course how we take our first language in.

There is something about that melding of reality and language which is not completely duplicable in one's relationship to a second language. It's this unconscious imbibing of the language. However: in order to understand poetry you must go on to understand this rift between the word and the moon.

George Szirtes:

I'll try to answer, very naïvely, Jon's question about what is the difference between writing and therapy, or the experience of therapy and writing. My answer is twofold. In writing you are engaged in a completely different kind of discourse. In writing, you have to deal with the history of writing, rather than the history of the self. Secondly, one is engaged with the world and the other is engaged with the self. Self diminishes in the literary project, quite often it completely disappears – it wants to know more about the world outside it than itself. It knows itself all too well.

Ogaga Ifowodo:

To return to the notion of exile, I've lived all my life in Nigeria and until 2001 I hadn't stayed outside Nigeria for longer than six months. Then I went to Cornell to do an MFA. I had been only two years in the US when somebody referred to me as an exile. I wrote back to say I am not an exile; I'm here to study. A huge debate followed; all these metaphorical meanings of exile came up. I really couldn't stand it. Let's not diminish the experience of exile. You are banished from your homeland – it is like political death. Without a passport, you are officially dead, as W.H. Auden bluntly put it. I'm not going to say that we shouldn't use exile as a metaphor, but I think we should be more careful.

Luisa Valenzuela:

While living in New York during the Argentine dark period, critics there insisted in categorizing me as an exile, and I insisted I was simply an expatriate for I had left my country voluntarily, and neither the situation nor the feeling could be compared. Two years before that, while lecturing in Mexico, the police entered my house in Buenos Aires, searching for me, and I was advised not to return for many months till the road was cleared. So I knew then how it felt to be an exile, and it is devastating. I suppose Eva is a real exile.

Eva Hoffman:

No, I'm feeling slightly defensive because there was only so much that I could say and I was using shorthand. I was using the notion of exile as a kind of illustrative device because that kind of transcultural movement has been very formative for me. I completely agree – we should not romanticize exile either as a difficult condition or a radical condition.

My kind of emigration was closer to exile because it was during the Cold War when one thought that you could never go back. Joyce, I suppose, did say: silence, exile and cunning. He also said it was Ireland that hurt him into writing and I kept thinking that we all need to be prodded or hurt into writing by something. Sometimes it's countries, sometimes it's certain kinds of losses.

I would like to expand on what George was saying about the difference between writing and psychoanalytic discourse. It seems to me that what writing can very uniquely do is to place subjectivity within the world. It can show the interaction of the two; it can show us subjectivity both as it is formed and constructed by the world, and as it perceives the world.

Ron Butlin:

I was just going to give another little spin to the question of language. I come from Scotland and I have two languages. In Scotland, most people have two, some three languages. Which language you choose to write in very much determines how you are going to live. If you write in Gaelic, spoken by a diminishing population of 14,000 or 15,000, you're going to get lots of subsidies. Much more is published in Gaelic – it'd never be published if it was written in English. If you write in Scots the same thing is going to happen except no one will read it. If you write in English, and publish in English having already written in Scots, you're labelled a betrayer. At the same time, all of us are kept out of the London publishing loop. So, there are other kinds of exiles.

Alison Croggon:

I think there needs to be a distinction between exile and emigration. Emigration is so much a fact of life, particularly in the last century with its huge shifts in population. Without all the baggage of exile, emigration is still a condition which can represent the most enormous psychic cultural shock. In his book *And Our Faces, My Heart, Brief as Photos* John Berger says that emigration involves not only leaving behind, crossing water, living among strangers, but also undoing the very meaning of the world and, at its most extreme, abandoning oneself to the unreal, which is the absurd. This is something I felt very strongly.

Kapka Kassabova:

I'm Bulgarian by birth, and I emigrated to New Zealand as a teenager. People in New Zealand were very keen to label me as an exile. I left Bulgaria in 1990, just after the fall of the Berlin Wall, so I'm not an exile but an economic migrant. I had to fight this label. It has occurred to me that now, after the fall of the Berlin Wall and the collapse of various dictatorships in South America, the true exiles of this world are actually fewer. Perhaps there is a kind of hunger for exiles, for this ideal of the person who is displaced, who is somehow better than us, even heroic. There is a need to exile, to exile ourselves, to take on the posture of exile.

For many years I convinced myself that my literary inheritance began with African-American women writers. They were my greatest influence because the beginnings of my writing career and my introduction to their work happened in tandem. As a younger woman when I sought other writers as role models, I had to cast my desperately seeking eye over the Atlantic and it was the writings of Toni Morrison, Alice Walker, Gloria Naylor, Michelle Cliff, Audre Lorde and others who sustained me.

I was raised with both my parents, a Nigerian father and a white English mother, in a predominantly white suburban London environment, but little of my father's Yoruba culture was passed on to me, not his language or food or traditions as such. I went to a school of 500 girls where I was all but the only black pupil for most of my time there. Sure I liked the Jackson Five but I just adored Donny Osmond. I didn't feel very black and I certainly wasn't white. So what was I in the polarized society of the time? I knew I didn't quite fit in but I didn't have the vocabulary to express it. This all changed when I left school and started learning about black cultures. At some point I had an epiphany and realized that during my childhood I had been deprived of learning about the African side of my heritage. This prompted my primal scream period, which lasted for several years, I have to say. I stamped my feet about an education system which saw no literary value in any writings by people of colour and most writing by women. As a consequence, I proceeded to block out everything that had preceded my introduction to African-American writing. Shakespeare? Dickens? Who were they? They had nothing to do with me nor I them. I was on another mission altogether.

To look at it with hindsight, I can see that I was balancing the scales. In looking for fiction that explored the existence of women in the African Diaspora I was looking for myself. And where were we in British fiction? Nowhere that I could see. Later I discovered the then recondite novels of writers who had first been published in the 1950s and 1960s such as Samuel Selvon, Wilson Harris, George Lamming (all from the Caribbean), and others such as Wole Soyinka and Chinua Achebe from Nigeria. But their novels featured few female protagonists, which was problematic for me. One notable exception was Buchi

Emecheta from Nigeria whose first novel *Second-Class Citizen* was about a Nigerian single mother living in London.

People who are in the majority in the society often do not understand this need for validation. Over the years I've heard such people say, sometimes rather superciliously, 'I don't read fiction to see myself in it'. Well neither do I *now*, but don't we look for writing that explains ourselves to ourselves when we're younger? Writing that expands who we are and how we can be in the world during those me, myself and I teenage years, which hopefully most of us grow out of. When the gap between our own cultural backgrounds and those portrayed in literature is a chasm, we can fall into it, screaming, sometimes silently, sometimes noisily, as I did. You see, I loved literature but I had discovered that literature, it seemed, did not love me.

Out of all the art forms, fiction and poetry are perhaps the most fertile imaginative ground for the in-depth examination and interpretation of our emotional, psychological, spiritual and intellectual landscapes; it helps us understand who we are and how we behave. I had grown up in a time where images of people of colour were mostly invisible in the UK. This was before the days of Benetton ads, Big Brother and multi-culti TV programming, black Members of Parliament and Alek Wek and Naomi Campbell as images of beauty. In my local library there were no books by black authors, and at drama school no plays either. To spot a black face on a British soap opera was a subject of discussion the next day and if we made it into the newspapers it was inevitably in a negative context. The cumulative effect was one of almost total invalidation by the society at large.

I discovered that literature did love black women in the novels and poetry of African-American women writers. Writing that honoured the intricate and complex web of human emotions, which revealed a rich range of human experience. Toni Morrison reigned as my literary queen because of her ability to create ordinary characters who are revealed as extraordinary; because of her insights, her empathy, her imaginative breadth and emotional gravitas, her suspenseful plots, and the ways in which she brilliantly evokes both the quotidian and the remarkable through such dense, textured diction. And how could Alice Walker's heart-rending *The Color Purple* not have a profound impact on those who read it? This American literature was incredibly affirming at first. But in time I realized that everything they wrote just seemed so much more complete, more terrible, more beautiful, more savvy, more sorted, more sassy and sensual and just so much more important than anything I could attempt. It was overwhelming. At first I wanted to write like them. Then I realized I couldn't. We were worlds apart. They were writing out of an African-American tradition, drawing on their own unique history, their cultural specificities, their many regional vernaculars. It wasn't mine. None of it was. I'd ask myself who on earth would want to read about a mixed-race girl growing up in a devastatingly dull suburb of Woolwich in South East London as I did, when they could read the stunningly luxuriant texts of Morrison, Naylor or Walker with their steaming swamps, slaves escaping through forests, their smouldering hick towns and dusty roads cutting through corn fields or cane fields, their rickety-shack houses peopled with ghosts and secret family histories, their colloquialisms which my *Sarf East Lundun-isms* didn't come anywhere near for downright coolness.

Over time, however, I became more circumspect about the effect this literature was having not only on me but on the literature of the UK. British publishers inherited the African-American literary success story and re-published over here; they were loath to publish homegrown black British fiction because they said there was no market for our work. This is hard to believe now but it was the case as recently as the early 1990s. I was beginning to feel diminished by the weight of this American literature. Influence was becoming a burden which was a bloody great sack of coal on my back. For a while I buckled under. Then I began to discover my own literary voice, or rather, multiplicity of voices, and thankfully there was nothing American about it. I wrote a novel-in-verse called *Lara* about seven generations of a mixed-race English/Nigerian London family (yes, living in the wonderful steaming swamps of Woolwich) with roots in Ireland, Nigeria, Brazil and Germany. Over 150 years, different characters pick up the family history in different eras and continents. Next came another novel-in-verse called *The Emperor's Babe* about a black Roman girl called Zuleika living in Londinium nearly 2,000 years ago. In 2005 I published *Soul Tourists*, a novel-with-verse about a mismatched couple travelling by car across Europe and featuring ten ghosts of colour from European history including Pushkin, Alessandro de' Medici and Mary Seacole. *Soul*

Tourists juxtaposes prose, poetry, prose poetry, scripts and non-literary devices such as a relationship row described through budgets.

The sack of coal was long ago dumped down a coal chute.

What I inherited above all else from these Americans was the confidence to write out of my own experience, *initially*, and to have faith in my choice of subject matter and style of writing, whatever that was. I could do my own thing and that was all right, thank you very much. This was a lesson a long time in the learning and I have been doing my own thing ever since. More recently I had another epiphany. *Of course* my influences went deeper, as far back as Ancient Greek drama. I'd so enjoyed Sophocles' plays *Electra, Oedipus the King* and the rebellious heroine Antigone. *Antigone* is still one of my favourite books of all time. Yes, it's a play, but it is also poetry and the words leap off the page as if in performance. With hindsight I can see the influence of Antigone on my novel-in-verse *The Emperor's Babe* which is, in part, very performative. One is ancient Greek, the other is ancient Roman. Both star young women battling with authority and both eventually die because of that battle, although Zuleika has much more fun *en route* to death than poor Antigone, with her camp transvestite friend Venus, her slapper girlfriend Alba and her extra-marital affair with the hunky Roman emperor Septimius Severus. And didn't I just love Chaucer's *The Canterbury Tales* with his wicked portrayals of very flawed, entertaining characters. To mention Shakespeare may be clichéd but how could I not have been influenced by his larger-than-life, typically complex, morally ambiguous, sometimes comic characters, the passionate intensity of his plays and sonnets, by his use of imagery to honour and enrich the complexities of his themes? Of course I'm not comparing myself to the Bard but I create big, morally ambiguous characters and I love figurative language. And wasn't I the brat who read the Victorian poet Tennyson's *Morte d'Arthur* very loudly every night for months before I went to sleep when I was 14? I relished the drama of the tale, the gorgeous alliterative sound patterning and, above all else, the sound of my own booming melodramatic voice, while my poor younger sister, trying to sleep in the bed opposite me, foamed at the mouth and rushed downstairs to complain to our mother. And wasn't I the nascent actress who played Captain Cat in the school production of the Welsh poet Dylan Thomas's poetic drama *Under Milk Wood* which he described as a 'play for voices'? I loved the play and now see its influence in the way in which I capture snapshots of many characters, in *Lara* in particular, and the poetry of my BBC radio verse-play *Madame Bitterfly and the Stockwell Diva*. Surely all of these poets and playwrights have been the source of my preoccupation with the conflation of poetry and storytelling in the novel-in-verse form, and even in my use of scripts in the novel-with-verse form of *Soul Tourists*.

You see, the fire was lit long before I encountered African-American writing. But I'd reduced this influence to ashes and blown it away.

I have not been overly influenced by African literature, as yet, although some people say they can see the influence of Soyinka, for example, in my writing, which is wishful thinking on their part. I've actually been more influenced by Bruce Chatwin's novel *The Viceroy of Ouidah*, about a slave trader based in Dahomey. Although politically I find the novel really dodgy, I find his succinct storytelling skills and stunning prose so original and exciting. When I was writing *Lara* I kept returning to two books for inspiration: Chatwin's and *Midsummer*, a sequence of sonnets by my favourite poet Derek Walcott.

My literary inheritance is obviously an ongoing story. Sometimes I think that everything I read and like is part of my literary tradition. (Yes, it's very selective). It all goes in and has to come out somewhere. I could list all the books I've loved in the past ten years: *English Passengers* by Matthew Kneale, *The Poisonwood Bible* by Barbara Kingsolver, *The Remains of the Day* by Kazuo Ishiguro, *Independent People* by Halldor Laxness, *Texaco* by Patrick Chamoiseau, *A Complicated Kindness* by Miriam Toews, *All That Blue* by Gaston-Paul Effa. I could go on. Maybe in 20 years' time I'll be citing the above as key influences in my literary heritage.

Both as a reader and a writer, one looks for the support of literary tradition. I was born shortly after the publication of *One Hundred Years of Solitude* so for me and the writers of my generation in Latin America, everything was far too easy. We grew up with those classics in our libraries: the works of Gabriel García Márquez, Mario Vargas Llosa, and Carlos Fuentes. We found ourselves everywhere in the literature we were reading. It was the 1960s – the time of the huge boom in Latin American fiction. We didn't have any trouble recognizing ourselves, our history and our tradition in the literature which was being written by Peruvian, Mexican, Colombian and Chilean writers. We didn't have to go too far to find ourselves.

The problem was that after some years, something started changing with that tradition and those models. We were quite concerned. All of a sudden we didn't recognize ourselves in Latin American fiction. Now, rather than referring to tradition, I'd like to describe it as a breakthrough or a change of direction in Latin American fiction that had been going on for some years.

I don't know how familiar American or European writers are with this change. Let me give some examples of what writers of my generation in Latin America have been writing recently. *In Search of Klingsor* by Jorge Volpi takes place in Germany and Denmark shortly after the Second World War. The characters are American and German and there's no reference whatsoever to Latin America. Argentinean writer Rodrigo Fresan has just published a book with a very Latin American title: *Kensington Gardens*. It's about the creator of Peter Pan. Some of my own novels take place in the Balkans, while my short stories take place in Pakistan, India, China.

How did this change happen? Why did it happen? We had the wonderful tradition of Latin American writers who had already shown us that they could write about Latin America and produce not only imitations of European novels but also very original novels like *One Hundred Years of Solitude*. I think that this very recent and dramatic change has to do with the exhaustion of that tradition. I refer to it as the moment 'when Latin American writers stopped feeding their iguanas to make them look like dinosaurs.' I think it has to do with an illness called 'magical realism'.

We were very fortunate to have the wonderful masters of Latin American fiction. We were unfortunate enough to assist in the decline of that fiction after a huge and all too easy success. Everything started to become exotic. If I were to give name to this discussion, I would refer to it as 'the risks of exoticism as a literary value.' After García Márquez, we understood that he and Fuentes had written realist novels: they had found a way to express our reality in an original way and they produced wonderful universal novels. After them, however, came a series of writers who forgot this universal tradition; the more local the novel seemed the better it sold and the more popular it became. We had to read these Latin American novels which were intentionally magical realist.

The label of 'magical realism' was invented in America. Latin American writers decided that they should tell everybody else how magical we were. They forgot that, for a reader such as myself, the novels of D. H. Lawrence and Jane Austen could also be very magical. A British rugby match can be absolutely magical. There was this very patronizing idea of Latin American writing which started to produce very strange fiction. Examples include Isabel Allende's *The House of Spirits* and – the most obvious – Laura Esquivel's *Like Water for Chocolate*.

In 1992, the Frankfurt Book Fair was dedicated for the first time to Latin American literature – Mexican literature to be precise. We were already starting to write our first short stories and novels at the time. *Like Water for Chocolate* was deemed to be the best example of Mexican fiction. We were absolutely appalled that Latin American fiction should be represented by ghosts and flying priests and such like. Mexican and Latin American writers were expected to write in that way. And, obviously, we didn't like the idea. We thought that García Márquez had written wonderful novels but we also had another writer who was a master of all this: Jorge Luis Borges. Without Borges, there would be no literary tradition in Latin America, or that tradition would have been completely different; yet Borges didn't write about Latin America.

So, in the mid-1990s, we understood that the homeland for the writer is not language, not nation, but the library. Our libraries contained Latin American fiction, including Borges obviously, but they also included Nabokov. Mostly, however, and this is very important, they included British fiction of the 1980s. We have one of the great examples with us here. Graham Swift probably won't remember, but in 1994 I interviewed him and many other writers who had been associated with the Latin American tradition. I asked them how they felt about the idea of magical realism. Fortunately, they were not very comfortable with that question, because magical realism was already démodé. Writers of my generation felt that the real Latin American tradition had been taken up by the British and European writers who had read *One Hundred Years of Solitude* or *The Death of Artemio Cruz*. They had understood that all these magical realities could take place anywhere. The tradition left Latin America, came back to Europe, and then we picked it up again from Europe. We started to write novels which have more to do with *The Remains of the Day* by Kazuo Ishiguro than with any novel written by a Latin American writer in the 1970s or the 1980s.

I hope, or I think, that writers in Latin America will eventually go back to writing about Latin America but this is not a must. We do not feel that we need to write about it anymore. We don't think we need to look Latin American. In Europe, and particularly in the UK, you are used to diversity, but in Latin America we are less diverse. There are four hundred million Latin Americans but we speak Spanish, writers usually come from the middle class, they grow up in Catholic or ex-Catholic families. So you can see there's no big diversity. That makes us feel that we don't need to be Latin American but rather just write the best way we can and pick up any tradition – our homeland is the library.

We don't deny the importance of the majority of writers of the Latin American boom and I think that they were more universal than they thought. They were referring to Latin America but, if you think of *One Hundred Years of Solitude*, you understand that it was much more than Latin American. This is my personal experience but I must say that it's also the experience of almost every Latin American writer born in the 1960s and 1970s. I don't know what will happen next. People now think that Latin American writers write only about the Second World War. It's another label. They say that Latin American authors no longer write about Latin America and that they have also turned to the 'exotic'. They write about Germans, Brits, Indians, about Chinese people. But that doesn't matter because the world we live in has that wonderful advantage that we can feel at ease wherever we go, and write about wherever we want.

Expectations, Inheritances and Literary Freedom

In conversation: Lisa Appignanesi, Christopher Bigsby, Ron Butlin, David Constantine, Jon Cook, Alison Croggon, Bernardine Evaristo, Moris Farhi, Choman Hardi, Eva Hoffman, Ogaga Ifowodo, Tessa de Loo, Ib Michael, Ignacio Padilla, Graham Swift, Dubravka Ugresic, Luisa Valenzuela and A.B. Yehoshua

Luisa Valenzuela:

I was upset with the notion of geography in writing, in the literal sense. Bernardine was referring to feelings, a way you see the world, not what part of the world you are looking at, or speaking from. I think we all have a very different way of focusing on reality, according to our grammar. Latin American writers, chiefly Argentines, are marked by Borges, not by García Márquez. A more universal way of seeing things has to do with our position in language, not with the place we are speaking from. I have written novels set in New York, even Barcelona. Many Argentine writers have written novels that are set in Paris, a city that embodies our fantasies. They are very different from novels written by New Yorkers or Parisians because we inhabit language from a different position.

Heidegger's old house of language has so many rooms! So many inhabitants. At times I feel invaded by different languages. They are not always welcome guests; they might push us to say things that seem to come from nowhere, perhaps from language itself. 'Write what you don't know about what you know' was Grace Paley's recommendation to her workshop students. It can be thrilling, and awesome.

Lisa Appignanesi:

We talked about Latin American fiction and African fiction, but I think in Britain we see Europe as not having a European fiction, though we often particularize the countries. I wonder what constitutes Latin America – is it a literary tradition? Is there really that much similarity between the individual countries within Latin America that actually constitutes this idea? Is it an opposition to America?

Ignacio Padilla:

If you refer to the Argentinean literature, it's a very specific writing, very different historically from the rest. But I think that the United Kingdom itself is so diverse, it's incredible. We don't have that diversity in Latin America. Probably it is because the literature in indigenous languages has started to appear only very recently, otherwise it's mostly literature in Spanish, influenced by Spanish and European models. I don't think the differences between Spanish literature and Latin American literatures are huge. It is almost the same tradition.

Bernardine Evaristo:

I don't want to homogenize Africa. People talk about it as if it is a single entity when it is a continent of 52 countries. I should really have said 'fiction from African countries.' It was merely a shorthand. The fiction I was referring to does come from different parts of the continent.

David Constantine:

I think that for writers beginning to write poetry in Britain today – since the collapse of any notion of Queen's English – Queen's English is spoken now only by the Queen – and the abandonment of Received Pronunciation – a huge variety of vernaculars is on offer. In the poetry being published in Britain now, and indeed over the last 10 or 15 years, there are very many and very different voices.

There is much insularity in England itself, but the poetry scene is wide open and in it many different and often contradictory styles and interests coexist. That seems to me a wholly good thing. I feel heartened not only by the poetry scene in the UK, but also by the work of translators and also – once you get beyond or below the great multinational presses – by what is being published and promoted. For writers and translators the UK is quite a lively place to be.

Dubravka Ugresic:

I just wanted to say that a completely new notion of literature is in circulation today. It is, more and more, 'world literature'. Though nobody knows exactly what 'world literature' means, there are many examples in different parts of the world. How does it work?

There is another phrase in circulation, connected with exile – 'writing out of nation'. It can be taken literally: you are writing in some other place, or in some other language, or simply about some other areas. We are probably all pushed towards that kind of resistance. You were talking about not fitting into the image that is imposed on us as writers – what we are expected to do by the manufacturers. The publishing industry likes to push us into stereotypes: because you can't sell a product that doesn't fit in with the mass expectations, we are all pressured to stand firmly behind the stereotype. I, for instance, am expected to write about the Balkans. You are expected to write about flying priests. People who adhere to the stereotypes are rewarded. That's why you have so many examples of self-exoticizing literature. I am going to be what you expect me to be – that sells the best.

Another factor that provokes resistance is the conservative forces of national literature, which they also want you to fit. They are so aggressive in some areas of the world precisely because the whole concept of national literature is collapsing. There are two tendencies – people either resist or fit in.

I know a very amusing story about an Indian writer who was born in Calcutta but he came to Amsterdam, lived there for three years, and then moved to the United States. He is what you might call an 'East European freak'. He wrote a novel about Hungarian intellectuals in Budapest in the 1970s. Although he was probably translated into Hungarian, the reaction was: how dare he write a novel about that – what does he know? Of course, his English publisher probably pushed him to write something like *The God of Small Things* but from a male perspective. He told me, 'I'm writing my Russian novel about the siege of Leningrad from a female perspective.'

Ignacio Padilla:

One of the good things about magical realism is, I think, that those resistances are not coming from the market anymore thanks to novels like *The God of Small Things* or *Like Water for Chocolate*. Otherwise we wouldn't have *The Remains of the Day* or *The English*

Patient, or so many other novels that don't care about geographical settings anymore.

Dubravka Ugresic:

Influences migrate. Believe it or not, during the 1970s in Croatia, I was part of a generation that was referred to as 'the generation of Croatian Borgesians'.

Jon Cook:

I'm not surprised that we've come on to labelling and marketing and the extent to which, when you're beginning a writing career, you feel the pressure of a label put upon what it is you are going to write about. It's not just a matter of technique but also of the material about which you feel permitted to write. I would like to keep in play the story that Bernardine told us about the way in which she moved from one literary context to another. What was helping her write at one time, namely that African-American tradition – those extraordinarily powerful writers like Toni Morrison and so on – was, as she found after a while, stopping her in a way, or they were constraining her from having access to something that had as much to do with Shakespeare and Chaucer as it had to do with a literature that was branded ethnically.

Ogaga Ifowodo:

I wanted to elaborate on the theme of a writer's homeland being his library. I would think that someone like Derek Walcott is saying the same thing when he says the poet has not a nation but imagination. But how can you be universal without being local? What would being local mean to this generation of Mexican writers who think this way?

Ignacio Padilla:

I think you're always local. We think about a novel like *Pedro Paramo*, which is the most important Mexican novel in the tradition. It's a very local novel but it's also universal. The same thing happens with *One Hundred Years of Solitude*. You will always be local because you are your own memory.

Jon Cook:

Another question is the extent to which, when we're thinking about writers and the past – both the literary past and this idea of homeland being a library – this is something that we might choose or something that finds us out. To paraphrase that famous Marx comment, history weighs upon the minds of the living like a nightmare. Can you find analogies for that in terms of the literary past or are we seeking a more benign metaphor for that relationship? What chooses the writer and what does the writer choose?

Alison Croggon:

I come from a country that is obsessed with the idea of a national literature. People are constantly saying: what is Australian literature and what is it supposed to be? We have a major literary prize that actually states in the rules that an Australian book has to be about Australia. There have been a few arguments about that but it's generally accepted as a description.

In my own evolution, African-American writing has been incredibly important but I'm obviously not black. When I had my first child as a single mother and I felt confused, writers like Alice Walker and Audre Lorde were enormously important. I found their work liberating, just as a woman trying to find reflections in literature that were useful to me. I'm still really grateful for those influences.

Ron Butlin:

I'd like to be a bit more commonplace about this. I think if you're going into the universal you have to start with the particular. The particular is not necessarily Walter Scott or Stevens, it's the village I grew up in, the weather, it's the grass, it's the wind. It's these very physical things that formed me just as much as the intellectual and emotional food that I received from people and books. I do feel that if we write about anything that is not where we come from, we still write about it in a particular way that is informed by the person we are, who grew out of a unique landscape.

Tessa de Loo:

I would like to add something about the stereotypes people have when they think of Holland. For Dutch writers it is very hard to find an audience in other countries. Foreigners want us to show something which is, in their eyes, typically Dutch (painters like Rembrandt, Vermeer, Van Gogh and images of tulips). But for us these are subjects that easily become clichéd. That is perhaps why two successful books dealing with Dutch subjects in the Anglophone world have been written by foreigners: *Tulip Fever* by Deborah Moggach and *Girl with a Pearl Earring* by Tracy Chevalier. Neither written by a Dutch writer. In Holland these books were not as well received as elsewhere. It feels a bit like foreign writers 'stealing our treasures' and doing with them whatever they please, whereas for us, writing about our past or our painters is something very delicate that demands enormous know-how and originality.

Choman Hardi:

In the case of Palestine and Kurdistan, where there is a lot of resistance literature, having a voice and writing about your history and your struggles is very important. When there is peace, hopefully then we can move beyond that. I have written a lot about my Kurdish background and, I imagine, at some stage I will confront the expectation to carry on writing about that without wanting to anymore.

I met a Palestinian poet who said, 'Now all I know what to do is write about stones and shadows.' I think that it is very important. Yes, we are pressurised to write about certain things but we also choose at certain stages of our lives to write about them.

Eva Hoffman:

I was just wondering whether the development of a displaced writer doesn't mirror a national tradition when the specific, the national, is in vogue. In the first stage of displacement, the writer is obsessed with memory, reproducing the past, and the lost country. The next natural phase is to move to a more cosmopolitan, globalized, international or inclusive world-view. In terms of world literature, we are at that stage when it is in vogue to write about other places, not the local, but the exotic. I wonder whether we are going through a phase. What will the next phase be? Will we become more and more global?

Ib Michael:

The source of literature is literature. It's not sex, gender, colour of skin – it's literature. We wouldn't be able to write without having read *The Iliad*. When the dynamic forces of literature wear out, it is then that we feel what Jon called 'the pressure of the label'.

I get this wonderful feeling when I'm reading Murakami. His characters are always wearing sneakers and making spaghetti. These characters are so un-Japanese. A very dynamic force in writing comes from alienation. García Márquez was very influenced by Kafka's *Metamorphosis*. Every writer grows up feeling alienated from his own culture, his own parents. We find out that the reason why we write is because we have this strong impulse to find our way, to find our voice.

Ogaga Ifowodo:

If the sources of literature are literature, then I wonder if that includes oral literature? I personally do not see *The Iliad* as literature in a sense. I think Derek Walcott is trying to make that point in *Omeros*. He's seeing Homer as an oral poet while he himself is writing in a literary tradition – he's making that move. I would like to know if tradition passes on from oral to written.

As an African I would like to say that the existence of an African diaspora has always made it necessary for us to have a cosmopolitan view or perspective.

Moris Farhi:

I come from Turkey. Turkey has been part of many cultures, as a result of which, as a kind of osmosis, we can easily move from one culture to another. There's a wonderful element of cultures leaking into each other and creating something quite new. Because there has been a great deal of persecution of writers in Turkey, as well as in South America where magical realism emerged in part to bypass censorship, magical realism was a way of telling a story.

Eva Hoffman:

I would like to introduce another word that kept coming to mind as I was listening. The word is freedom – artistic freedom. Of course, it is an aspect of the writer's condition and of imaginative writing in particular that there is an enormous amount of freedom in it. You can create your library, you have access to so many environments and diversities. We've been talking mostly about tradition in the use of certain kinds of identities. Of course, there are traditions in the service of form and the creation of a voice, and of grappling with questions of language. There again we have so much freedom. At the same time artistic freedom is not a given. The other polarity we were talking about is represented by certain kinds of restraints.

I'd just like to insert this idea of freedom and mobility. One use of literature, tradition and the past is, in a sense, to decode and understand one's own consciousness. I sometimes see writing as an attempt at catching one's own consciousness, one's own time, one's own place. Catching it by the tail, so to speak – catching it as much and as richly as possible.

Aside from the question of expectations – are we expected to write the national literature, to conform – it seems to me that the world is becoming both more cosmopolitan and more national. We need to catch this moment in which we are of particular cultures and yet live in a very mobile world.

David Constantine:

One way or another a writer must come into his or her own voice. A lot of reading is needed to bring you into a voice in which you can actually say those things that matter to you. You need to learn what your language has done, and what it still can do. Whether the sonnet, which has been around in Europe for 700 years, can still be written, and how. What an elegy looks and feels like, how it works, in our modern English. Are epigrams feasible? Is an epic poem? If so, how would you manage it? You learn by reading what your language has done thoughout its history and what it is still capable of doing, properly modified into modernity. That's why I said earlier that the British poetry scene is encouraging. It's not just a variety of voices that are on display and in use, there's also a great variety of possible forms.

Every writer is somewhere in the language's tradition. It is not possible to be nowhere. And it is not possible for a poem to have no form. But that form may be more or less pleasing, more or less effective. It's as well to sort out soon what language can still be done, and in what form. That's the way that reading helps the writer. You begin with something as local as Ron's village – the wind and all the rest of it – and from what your language has already done.

Graham Swift:

A thought about this question of how literature can produce literature. Obviously it does: all writers are influenced by other literature. But I don't think it's quite as simple. Someone said earlier that we are all divorced from our childhoods. I don't know if I agree with that. What I'm coming round to say is that one of the most influential things in my writing were the first things I read. They were things that I read as a child. Things that I can't remember now. I certainly didn't think at the time that they were literature. In fact, some of them might have been quite badly written books but they put me under the spell of storytelling. I still maintain that it was that very early reading, from the age of five, that somehow filtered through. My earliest sense of wanting to be a writer was like wanting to be an engine driver. I read these writers and thought, 'how wonderful to do that – I want to be one of those.' That came very early in my life and not from what I would call literature.

Christopher Bigsby:

Mario Vargas Llosa's explanation for magical realism was that the novel was banned for 300 years in Latin America. Therefore the fiction-making impulse was deflected into all other aspects of society: politics, religion, social life. Thus, magical realism, when it emerged, was realism. It simply reflected the fictionalizing of the culture. On another point, Alfred Kazin said that 'cosmopolitanism was Jewish parochialism.' It's a teasing thought. I wonder if it isn't becoming a new parochialism for writers. The emerging transnational aspect is being favoured, certainly in academe. I went to a conference in the United States of an American Studies association which a few years ago had lost confidence in there being such a thing as America, to such an extent that it actually proposed its own dissolution! All papers were on transnational writers or they were on the Native Americans or the American Hispanics. I asked if it was possible to think that there could have been a paper on Philip Roth on the grounds that he was Jewish and came from a minority and they said, 'We don't mean that kind of minority.'

There is a new fashion within academe, which is precisely to be receptive to those who inhabit nowhere, because if you inhabit nowhere, you're at home. It's like going to New York – since everyone is a stranger, you're at home. It's the only city that I know of in which taxi driving is regarded as an entry profession. There are people who drive taxis in New York with a mental map of Omsk. In some ways there is a literature there that anyone can unearth, precisely because it refuses its particularities.

I was a judge of a Singapore literary prize and I gave it to somebody who was born and raised in Singapore, educated in England, lived in New York and wrote a book called *Man and Ink*, which is absolutely a novel of today, the kind of novel that is indeed being favoured. I wonder whether we are starting to create our own version of parochialism, which is precisely a world literature.

Dubravka Ugresic:

This question is extremely complex. You were talking about imagery and fashions. I do think that world literature or transnational literature is very fashionable, but I also think that the model of national literature still prevails everywhere. If you think about cultural or literary geopolitics, you can't avoid seeing that there are major literatures and literatures whose languages do not matter much. They might be welcome like a nice but strange dish, Indonesian or Nigerian, for example, but the communication is not equal or reciprocal.

Writers write in order to communicate, and communication implies negotiation of means. I can't speak to you from the position of national literature. You can speak to me because Shakespeare is a world writer. In order to communicate and be visible I have to skip my national references. I can't write a postmodern piece relying on my national literary sources because you would not understand it, but I can play, as a foreigner, with English literary tradition because everybody understands it.

Writing Worlds 1
The Norwich Exchanges

Writing and Place

I am four years older than the State of Israel; I'll probably die before the Israeli occupation army withdraws from my country. A lifetime of exile left me with incurable displacement and unstoppable memory. Memory is residence in time. When I was given permission to visit my country after 30 years of life in the countries of others, I did not want to relive the landscape but to recover my moments in it, 'to sew patches of time together, I want to attach one moment to another, to attach childhood to age, to attach the present to the absent and all presents to all absences, to attach exiles to the homeland and to attach what I have imagined to what I see now.' (*I Saw Ramallah*).

Place is a term that has an unlimited range of associations and functions. Think how a dot on the map can come amazingly and passionately alive, saturated with diverse nuances and connotations. Place points to what happened and what is happening and what will happen. It points to regional or national identity, a special location, a cultural frame or structure, to spongy nostalgia and romanticized melancholy and, in certain cases, it points to geographical entitlement i.e. conflict and aggression. These are not definitions of place, for we have as many definitions of the term as the disciplines we choose, ontological or metaphysical or aesthetical etc., but more than 30 years of *displacement* have taught me to see place as *time*.

I lived in more than 30 flats in several cities in three continents; as if the rooms, the walls, the streets, the restaurants, the airports and train stations, the offices and the landscapes of exile were made up of memories and would always generate memories. Though solid, concrete and necessary, I have never dealt with those places as final or lasting. The lack of free choice, the sense of temporality, and the fact that I am forced to be here or there against my free will brought with it anger not nostalgia.

A place can be defined and redefined endlessly according to lived experience. In the past five years, 69 pregnant Palestinian women had to give birth to their babies at Israeli military checkpoints. They were denied access to hospitals. To the woman who was forced to give birth near the boots of Israeli teenagers in uniform, the meaning of a bed in the maternity hospital or at home, is different; to the child whose future life is likely to be threatened every day as it was threatened on the first day, the meaning of a *birthplace* will never be the same. On the other hand, children's success in getting to their classrooms through mountainous detours, bypassing the military checkpoints, becomes a triumphant moment. It is the shape of our moments in a place that really counts and it is by these moments that a place is redefined. Execution chamber and the honeymoon hotel are places; a city to two lovers preparing to go out for a candlelit dinner is not the same place as to a hiding fugitive chased by his enemies that very night. One person's dream place can be the nightmare of another and a location that brings with it neutral feelings to some, can bring the sharpest associations to others e.g. Vietnam, Robben Island, Bethlehem, Abu Ghraib etc.

My book *I Saw Ramallah* is not about Ramallah, it is about my times in it, without it, away from it, because of it, in spite of it and on the way to it. Occupation destroys cities and distorts the place with barracks, checkpoints, barbed wires, noises and blood. Cities might rise and resist, might retaliate and be restored, but the real tragedy is that occupation destroys Time and distorts its shape, and Time cannot be re-owned or retrieved. For an exiled person, time grows outside its natural soil, like a plant whose roots are hung in the air.

For a place to be a place, however, we have to be able to move in it, to it and from it. When such ability is denied, the place acquires different meanings – it becomes a symbol and an identity. The Berlin Wall and the Israeli Wall cannot be looked at as sites, they are concepts and judgments. Place is like childhood, it is not a mass or a structure which stands outside us or which we leave behind, it keeps functioning throughout all stages of life in our actions and reactions. I am inundated, not by the *dream house* of Gaston Bachelard, but by the factual temporality of all my other houses. The remote, cloudy place is, paradoxically, restored in words that are condensed, specific and solid. Be it poetry or prose, this necessarily leads to conceptual exactness and precision. A place becomes an idea not an ideology, that's why I do not praise everything in my homeland and I do not criticize everything in exile. 'The vagrant holds on to nothing. The one whose will is broken lives in his own internal rhythm. Places for him are means of transport to other places, to other conditions, as though they were wine or shoes.' (*I Saw Ramallah*).

Someone said here that displacement might not be bad for a writer in the age of globalization. This of course is understandable in case of free will and personal choice, but let me say that displacement is totally and completely different for a person with a broken will or for a large part of a nation, those millions who become unwelcome refugees.

The cruellest aspect of displacement is that it makes us strangers not only in the outside world but also among our own people. When I returned to my village accompanied by a relative, I found myself nodding and smiling as he introduced me to people I was supposed to know quite well; of course I did not know who they were and had to pretend I did. The failure to recapture the intimacy has redefined the whole place. 'Life does not allow us to consider repeated uprootings as tragic, for there is an aspect to them that reminds us of farce, and it will not allow us to get used to them as repeated jokes, because there is always a tragic side to them. The person on a swing gets used to moving in two opposite directions; the swing of life carries its rider no further than its two extremes, farce and tragedy.' (*I Saw Ramallah*)

This absurdity in the relation with space on a personal level is to be doubled and more puzzling from a universal perspective. Let us just think of the following paradox: geographical explorations of the world and scientific discoveries of the human body led to the expansion of the physical world but resulted in the narrowest-minded discourses of colonialism, slavery and racism. Millions of innocent people suffered extinction and collective death; continents were robbed of their raw materials and natural resources; millions of humans were enslaved and uprooted and settlers or armies occupied distant countries. After a short period of relative international security, Earth, our common and only place, is now living in fear and uncertainty. The single-sided intolerant claims of truth with which the world is now ruled, and the ideology of terrorism, might take the planet to its destruction. The idea of sharing a space, the essential idea behind love, peace and justice, has never been as threatened as it is today. What would we gain if all the scientific achievements and explorations of mind resulted in such a wider space and such a narrower mentality?

Art probably comes at the top of human activities that open up closed worlds and make it possible to understand the experience of others in far away places and distant times. Art opens up space, it means space; the discourse of the present masters of the world closes the world, reduces it to 'us/them', to 'the good guys' – the ones who are *like us*; and 'the bad guys' – those who are *different*. This discourse means confinement, exclusion, reduction and, eventually, death.

The endeavour of poets, the guardians of individuality, has always been to articulate the complexity and diversity of human experience and to encompass and recreate our consciousness of our relation to the self, the other and the universe. Like meticulous craftsmen, they work to bring together the physical and the spiritual, the general and the particular, the conceptual and the palpable, the local and the universal; and the question comes out: what does it mean to have a planet with hundreds of races, cultures, styles, affiliations, languages and histories, all dominated by one power, one ideology and one judgment?

It was not Lotman who taught me the meaning of 'obstacles' and 'barriers' that made the space narrower but it was my everyday experience as well as that of my family and my people. Life has put me face to face with the following question: what happens when the place becomes the absence of the place? What happens when the difference between 'where' and 'when' is blurred or mixed? What happens when the painful 'here' becomes a dream of a pleasant 'elsewhere'? Such questions necessarily lead to the only answer – place is freedom. Isn't the concept of freedom mainly related to our lot in a certain place? The difference between the horizon and the prison cell is also a feeling. In some personal as well as national cases these two opposite places can be one and the same thing:

Man said:

Blessed are the birds in their cages
For they at least, know the limits
Of their prisons!

In conversation: Leila Ahmed, Lisa Appignanesi, Mourid Barghouti, Gillian Beer, Christopher Bigsby, Ron Butlin, Austin Clarke, David Constantine, Jon Cook, Alison Croggon, Vesna Goldsworthy, Choman Hardi, Kapka Kassabova, Hasso Krull, Graham Swift, George Szirtes, Dubravka Ugresic and A.B. Yehoshua

Leila Ahmed:

What Mourid Barghouti's essay puts very clearly on the table is that there is no extricating writing from politics. One can perhaps push it to the side of one's consciousness but these are the issues of our times and we cannot write anything outside of this context, whether we choose to recognize it or not. This is one of the great problems of our time.

That said, I cannot comment or expand on what Mourid has said. These are realities that you have to deal with daily as a writer. This is the place, in every sense of the word, from which you write. I won't comment – it's there for all of us to take up. Let me just pick up on the details, the margins. Mourid, you did refer to 'us' and 'them' and imperial power. One of the things I thought about as I was listening was the 'us' and 'them' divide. Certainly you are writing for two audiences who are in opposition. You are at the heart of this clash of civilizations. Somehow, you have to span two different audiences with presumably very different notions of the very issue which you are talking about.

As Dubravka has said earlier, there are expectations set for us by the audiences, publishers and packaging. You have different kinds of audiences and publishers. How do you negotiate that? Is there any hope of doing it?

Mourid Barghouti:

I don't think of my translations as a starting point. I come from a certain place and a certain history. I am made up of this geography and history. I developed a way of receiving the world, of trying to transmit it through creative writing. I'm a poet – I've published 13 collections of poetry and a collected works. And then my first prose book was suddenly picked up by Random House, by Bloomsbury, by everyone.

I never exert any effort to publicize my work. My relation with my text ends with the last line. My job ends there. I don't knock on the doors of publishers. I just try to create a work of art that is pleasing to me even when it is dealing with unpleasant stories. Reading should be a pleasurable process. The work of art should justify its elements. Whether it's long, short, classical, or experimental, the *raison d'être* of a work of art is its structure.

I opted to write in physical language. My translators and my publishers told me that the difference between the original and the translations into other languages – Spanish or French, for example – is really minimal. Every translator told me that such precise wording helped them as translators.

Leila Ahmed:

I was wondering, now you have a wide audience, like it or not, because you are translated into many languages: will this new audience be part of whom you are writing for or not? Earlier, somebody raised a question about an author not having women in their novel and reflected that this was a thematic issue: it is a work of art. Some of us have been questioning whether the notion of a work of art isn't itself a construct by some classes perhaps to exclude women or working-class aesthetics. The idea of a work of art is something that could be deconstructed or rethought or re-imagined in ways that are non-political.

Mourid Barghouti:

I would love women to be represented well in a work of art. Nizar Kabbani is a poet adored by everyone and often called 'the poet of women'. He is admired as a great defender of women and yet he is a male chauvinist. He writes about a woman who is unrecognizable: only mirrors, crystals, perfumes. You can't find her on any campus, she's not your cousin, she's not a student, she's not working in any field. He is a best-selling author. I have problems with this kind of fallacy. I just wanted to mention this as an example.

Don't tell me a novel is bad because it speaks about history, about women, about fantasy, about ghosts. The theme does not justify the work of art. The work of art must justify the theme. This is my point. There are noble themes and bad works of art. There are mean themes and great works of art. I never preface my poems with introductions in a reading. After all, they are works of art. Take it, rethink it, throw it away, love it – do with it what you want. The difference between a mediocre carpenter and a genius is the point at which they can say, 'it is finished'.

Jon Cook:

This idea of a work of art justifying every element within it is a profoundly important one. We were talking about place, however. I wonder, Leila, whether you had anything more to say? When Mourid made a very powerful statement about the vanishing of place in certain historical circumstances, he was also outlining a major crisis in the possibility of there being such a thing as place today. The idea of sharing a space has never been so threatened.

Leila Ahmed:

What is striking to me is the idea that history is a place. Mourid's experiences are different from my own life. There is an event, a place, a history, a huge construct within which he has to write. I don't have that. How confining or liberating is it? There is no escape for you; it is the missing story of the 20th century.

Mourid Barghouti:

I'm not the only one who is stateless.

Gillian Beer:

Something came up yesterday when you were reading. You read in English and yet translation has no meaning for you, as I understood it. To me, it seems that a poem is a place and that place is full of sounds, sonorities, echoes. What you offered to us, very moving though it was, was a displaced version of the poem that you have written. One thing I wondered was whether you happened to have beside you an Arabic original of any of the poems because it did seem to me that what we weren't receiving was that thickness of the experience. When you were referring to a work of art justifying itself through all its elements, the element of sound is so strong.

Mourid Barghouti:

I sometimes read a sample in Arabic, just to give the taste of the rhythm and voice and structure. When I'm not alone on the stage, I fear that I might be taking the time of others.

Choman Hardi:

Just to return to this idea of place. I'm familiar with a few Palestinian poets and the fact that you don't have a place on the map is as central to Palestinian writing as it is to Kurdish writing. I think many of us try to write that place, to make it. Every now and then, I'm still asked by someone, can you show that place to me on the map? My whole book is about trying to write this place, to make it happen.

I use some of Mourid's poems in my creative writing workshops. I had to search for them in *Banipal*. I think that was a central thing – writing a place, and the experiences that come from not having a state, the daily things as well as the bigger things.

Hasso Krull:

I also wanted to say a couple of words about place. The Palestinian question reminded me that Estonia became independent during the 20th century. The so-called Soviet occupation lasted 50 years. After the Soviet forces left, quite a number of places were freed in a physical sense. Military bases were left empty and buildings became ruins, with grass and young trees growing among them. In the 1990s, young artists started to devise all kinds of projects in those places, such as performance art and even exhibitions. When I attended these, I always wondered what was the strange force of attraction of those emblematic places to which access was prohibited during the Soviet times. They were surrounded with barbed wire and defended by armed men. Then the men left and, suddenly, those places about which we had no idea, besides the historical fact that the invader had been there, started to fascinate people. I think that perhaps there is also some kind of mirror effect, if one compares this to an older tradition of writing about place that existed in Estonian oral culture even in the 19th century.

Particular places in the countryside – stones, valleys, caves – were connected with all kinds of traditional narratives. Each village and community had those stories. They imbued places with meaning. Now my compatriots live in towns, the population is urbanized and this particular oral culture is extinct, although much of it has been recorded. After the Soviet occupation, there was this new fascination with those places marked only by the negative effect, by the absence of narrative, past and present.

Lisa Appignanesi:

John Berger once wrote a play called *A Question of Geography* about the Soviet camps. I find myself in a tricky situation addressing you now because I'm one of these people who was born, in a sense, lucky, because my geography didn't matter and I spent my life trying to leave states and not think about them too much. You've created the idea of statelessness as quite the opposite of how I consider it.

I wonder if statelessness can also be a place of virtue. In other words, as soon as you begin to talk about place and your particular statelessness I feel slightly ill at ease because I'm lucky. I've been lucky enough not to have this particular burden or this particular task, the project of having to create a state having been born into one that then went away or left me. So I don't know really how to respond to your sense of place because you both want it to be a virtue and a burden and also something very specific. I wonder how you would like us to feel about this?

Alison Croggon:

Is place the same as home? It seems to me that you're talking about home or a sense of what home is. Home as a place around a hearth, where some kind of sacred sense intersects with the quotidian. This is where we humanly create an idea of what a home is.

Mourid Barghouti:

I understand this remark. My book that tackles the theme of place is *I Saw Ramallah*. If you read it, you will see there's no glorification of home and no anger about the places of exile. If you idealize, you don't write well. No nostalgia at all. Nostalgia leads to spongy, wishy-washy language. Precision makes us avoid such creative mistakes. There's gratitude at being understood even in strange places.

The issue, however, is broken will. When your will is broken then the meaning of place becomes different. The meaning of time becomes different. The meaning of language becomes different. I mean, a broken will means that you want to go but you are not allowed. The broken will does not result in nostalgia or the glorification of the lost place. In the book, there's a lot of sarcasm and irony, even relating to the name of my family and the habits of the village.

A.B. Yehoshua:

From time to time, poetry is simplistic about things – this is bad poetry. You said that a work of art must be understood only by itself, but this is not right, because it also has to be understood in reference to reality, in reference to the moral values behind it. Poems which refer to reality have to be accurate about the way they present it and how much of it is entering the poem. Not seeing the other side can be very dangerous.

You spoke about the 69 Palestinian women who had their babies at army checkpoints: why have these checkpoints been created? They have not been created simply in order to torture women. They have been created in order to protect other people from terrorism. There are always two sides. A question is how a poem can see all these things. How can you enter the suffering of the other side without denying the sufferings of your people? This was raised by the Palestinian press, after the death of Arafat. It was also mentioned in our literature. The major portion of our writing has always been in opposition, against the government, but because we are living in a democratic society we could allow ourselves to be oppositional.

In a certain way, poetry can poison politics. We know of poets and writers who damage the concept of freedom. We know how much fascism there was in poetry. What were the poems in the Communist area? How much damage have they done to politicians and to people's concepts and ideas?

I cannot simply appreciate a poem because of its structure, its imagery or metaphors. I have to judge it also by how much it is relevant to what is good and what is bad, according to my ideas of good and bad.

Austin Clarke:

That is precisely the problem, I would say. Whose standards are you using in judging the poetry from different cultures and a different point of view?

Jon Cook:

I can see an obvious relationship between the debate that is arising and questions of place. We are talking about one of the major contestations over place that exists in the world today. It would be foolish to deny that. We are talking about what happens to the responsibilities and, indeed, the activity of writing in conditions of such fierce contestation.

What we haven't fully articulated is a situation where, in order for one set of people to have a place, another set of people can't and that is rather offensive to our notion that we might be living in a context where there is enough space to go around for everybody. If we want to speak democratically, there's a fundamental human right here – the right to have a place.

In relation to the question about judging a work of art that was posed by Austin, I think that there is an important respect in which works of art begin to provide the understanding and the terms within which they will be judged. Historically, with significant works of literature, we learn over time how to read them. Often the existing canons of taste and judgment are not able to comprehend what has happened. I do think it is important to, at least, keep hold of that idea.

There is a value, which Mourid is articulating, in a certain kind of autonomy. I'm thinking about the way that autonomy is connected to a notion of place. To be autonomous is, in a sense, to need, to require, to have a place of your own. In judging literary works, there's a constant dilemma that, it seems to me, most people want to get out of. On the one side, there is the idea that the work is to be justified with reference to a particular moral or historical responsibility it might have. We need to think seriously about the value of literature precisely in those terms. On the other hand, there's the advocacy of the idea that a work of art justifies itself in terms of some intrinsic formal properties: the way in which it is put together, the care with which language is used, and the form which is shaped out of that language. What happens, typically, is that people group around one side or the other. As Eva put it, 'in-between spaces' is where most people don't like to be. On the one hand you have to acknowledge the legitimacy of the work itself and, on the other, think about its ethical obligations – without one contaminating the other.

Christopher Bigsby:

I used to ask students who were applying to the university some questions to see how their minds were working. I would start with Kafka's *The Trial*. It didn't matter whether they'd read the novel or not, I would give them the story. Then I would say, 'what if I told you that Kafka was Jewish?' They would respond, 'Ah yes, you're arbitrarily picked out because you belong to a particular race.' 'What if I told you that he died of tuberculosis?' 'Ah yes, it's about how illness arbitrarily strikes you down', they would say.

Then I showed them a sonnet and asked them, 'would it make any difference if I told you it was by an American? Would it make any difference if I told you it was by a female American? Would it make any difference if I told you it was by a black female American?' Then I would say, 'would it make any difference if I told you it was by a black female slave?' And suddenly the word 'freedom' used in the poem changed. The fact that it was modelled upon English metrics had a kind of significance. The reference to 'salvation lying in a life beyond' suddenly had a meaning and an irony that it never had before.

The notion, which used to be popular, that a work of art is

washed up on the shore in a bottle and you know nothing of the culture it came from, is, I think, fallacious. It does not mean that you do not derive something from that work. There are problems. This is the reason I ask the students these questions – because there is no right answer. These are real problems, real challenges.

I teach American Studies. In order to locate that literature I have to go some way to constructing a culture from which this literature has come. Then we realize that we'd always assumed that you didn't have to do that with English Literature because it was in the bloodstream. Then we had to create English Studies, by analogy, because we realized it wasn't in the bloodstream. We're dealing with a generation that never read the Bible. I was in a class of 22 people, including several Americans, and I asked who had read the Bible; none of them had. How do I teach Melville or Milton? These writers come out of a world, a context. It is a complex, ambivalent negotiation you have to go through.

David Constantine:

We are not talking about art for art's sake when we call a work of art autonomous. Goethe's novel *Elective Affinities,* which was published in 1809, was reviled by half the public for undermining the institution of marriage, and praised by the other half for celebrating it. Goethe, defending himself against both camps, said that a literary work must insist on its own right to be, and on its own ways of being right. The work itself sets the criteria by which it can be judged. It is wrong to ask of a literary work that it be impartial or 'fair'. A novel is not a report by the Social Services. It might be one-sided, might (like Goethe's *Werther)* be a tunnel-vision, and yet be wholly sucessful and satisfying, by the criteria it sets itself.

Ron Butlin:

The readers bring their imagination, their uniqueness and their heritage and history to the poem or the story. For each reader the experience is very different.

Choman Hardi:

I think we can enjoy a work of art as it is without knowing its background, but I also think we will enjoy it more if we understand the context.

Jon Cook:

This takes us back to the question of place. The fascinating thing about strong literature is the way it supplies its own context. If I was to think about the difference between reading a sonnet by Shakespeare and a parish record drawn out of a late 16th-century church roll, it seems to me the work by Shakespeare carries more of its own context than the parish record and church register. I do think there is a special sense in which the form or properties of literature do allow it to move from one place and one time to another. These are all very abstract descriptions of what in practice are very real engagements with particular works at particular times. When I listened to Mourid's poetry, the fact that I was listening to a Palestinian poet writing about Palestine wasn't in the front of my mind. It didn't seem to me to be vital to the pleasure I got from the experience.

Christopher Bigsby:

Do I care if *Richard III* accurately reflects the historical situation? I don't give a damn. But the writer has the ability to transform places. Wordsworth and Coleridge have made the Lake District what it is, so now we cannot view those places innocently. We view them through a lens. There is John Fowles's Dorset. It has taken us a century to shake ourselves out of that version of London that has been offered by Dickens. There are tours taking you through a fictive city as though it were real. You could be taken through places inhabited by fictional characters. I once went with a television crew to film *Huckleberry Finn*. We wanted to film Jackson's Island. But Jackson's Island never existed! So powerful is this work of fiction that it has the ability to turn a place into something else.

Jon Cook:

The issue here is the idea that writing can create a place. I wonder how much we need to be able to live imaginatively. This goes back to the question of being at home, and whether it involves a dimension of imaginative investment. This takes on very strange articulations in contemporary culture. We have trips to real cities invested by the imagination of Joyce or Dickens. Through the power and ability of their writing, we identify the place. In a sense this is equal to baptism, giving the place a name. Then there is the question of utopia.

Christopher Bigsby:

Graham Swift is of course guilty – there are people wandering around East Anglia looking for the dead body in the water, as Graham has located it there for us.

Dubravka Ugresic:

Graham's works have really touched me because they are so poetical. I like their inner dynamics related to territory and landscapes etc. In my books places and towns also play a role. I have a book with an awful title – *Have a Nice Day*. It was called *My American Fictionary* in the original version, but my publisher thought nobody would understand that, as though readers are so stupid that they can't connect dictionary and fiction. The book has some American landscapes, mostly urban. My novel *The Museum of Unconditional Surrender* surrenders itself to Berlin, because Berlin perfectly matched my feelings and I wanted to express that. The title relates to the real place – the Museum of Unconditional Co-operation of Germany really existed in Berlin. It's about cultures – German culture and Russian culture and co-operation. The relationship between art/writer and place is complicated and mystical because we are usually chosen by places. We do not choose them.

I think the discussion of literature and art doesn't end with the statement that the work of art is autonomous. I don't think that writers have total freedom because you lose the freedom from the moment you start to write. Even when you are writing a letter, you

Conversation 61

are writing in a certain genre and tradition. Even when you are writing an email you are not free because you use the language already established, the code of communication. If you send a message on your mobile, you also use an established language. We all write within established codes. And literature is about codes. When we consider changing the place, or being translated, we also change our positions. Consciously or unconsciously, we bear our audience in mind, because we do send our messages to that audience. We do not send our messages to God and leave them on his answering machine. What I have observed lately is that when those systems crash, when national literatures do not function as houses any more, writers reposition themselves.

Graham Swift:

You said you can't choose your place. But I think you can. Of course, we can't choose where we are born. I am still very near the place where I was born. Writers can do what they do anywhere. Their job is what they are, they can choose to write anywhere. I am a suburban person, I had a choice and I haven't left suburbia, the most unexotic environment to inhabit. I like the anonymity of the suburbs. I can sit in the room in my suburb without needing spectacular views for my writing. There can be a way in which writers need such a neutral place. But I'm sure other writers would have a different view of things.

George Szirtes:

I would like Graham to say more about this in the context of the local. There must be some people who would recognize the Fens in your book, as much as they would recognize SW19. Where is your SW19 set as compared to the SW19 I may walk into?

Graham Swift:

Waterland is set in a place I didn't come from. It has become the exception. One of my theories is that I went into this novel with a totally naïve sense of place and setting. I thought then that place maybe doesn't matter, the setting doesn't matter. Of all English landscapes I chose the one that is most like an empty stage, as the Fens are very flat. Then I discovered my mistake, as the background of the Fens becomes almost the foreground. I think what I'm good at in my stories is the close-to-home territory. The uprooting isn't geographical, it comes from going into someone else's experience; the uprooting happens within a character. In some way that is more demanding than setting a novel in an unfamiliar environment.

Kapka Kassabova:

We don't have the choice of where we are born, but we do have a choice of pursuing a 'magical' landscape that we can relate to, and that rarely turns out to be our home. The place of my fantasy isn't in Bulgaria where I was born or in New Zealand where I emigrated to. I stayed in New Zealand for 12 years writing about other places. I set my first novel in Bulgaria and partly in New Zealand, and my second novel in Greece and France. For me, New Zealand became a safe place. Its landscape wasn't the landscape of my imagination, so I turned to others, imaginary or real. We invent places. We do have that choice. Our imagination provides it. I don't mean that in terms of beauty. I believe that we have a relationship with a landscape that we don't always find in our own lifetime. To look for a 'magical' place that brings me 'ecstasy, perhaps even death', in the words of Paul Bowles, is important to me.

Vesna Goldsworthy:

Graham, I don't think the suburbs are boring places, quite the opposite. I also believe that the rationale for choosing the Fens and the rationale for choosing suburbia are very similar as they both offer a sense of being at the margins, in a place where anything can happen. Which philosopher was it who said that the boundary isn't that where something stops, but where something begins its presencing?

Graham Swift:

Superficially, the whole point is to discover a story wherever you start. I don't think the suburbs are boring in that sense. The suburbs have some remarkable stuff.

Vesna Goldsworthy:

In both the British and American imagination, there is always that Gothic aspect in writing about the suburban.

Graham Swift:

There is the whole genre of travel writing where writers go to other places. Being a fiction writer is perhaps the opposite, because you travel in your head. When you travel and people in some foreign city ask, 'Do you like our city?', you are not going to say no. If they ask me, 'Do you think you are going to use it as the setting for your book?', instead of saying, 'Probably not' I say, 'I'll think about it.' But fiction writing for me isn't like a reconnaissance trip where you set out to claim places. The places in your book just pop up in your head.

George Szirtes:

You set up rules of the game according to which you want the book to be read; you decide to some degree what the reader could expect and whether they are or are not going to follow your book with their own map. If you choose realism, you make sure that you have made all the journeys that are in the book. If you are selling this kind of realism, then you are saying: here is the place I recognize. It is a game of conventions, isn't it?

Graham Swift *The Place of Place*

East Anglia is not a bad place for me to offer you some of my thoughts about place in fiction. Some years ago I wrote a novel called *Waterland*, which is set not just in East Anglia but in a particular and peculiar part of East Anglia known as the Fens. Ever since that novel was published quite a few people have assumed that I must have been born there or at least lived there for some time. The truth is that I have no personal connection with the region at all, other than the fact that I've set a novel there. For the record, I was born in South London and still live there, just a few miles in fact from where I was born. And, incidentally, a large part of *Waterland* is set in Greenwich.

When I'm forced to disabuse those people of their false assumption, they can sometimes be surprised; sometimes, oddly, rather disappointed; and sometimes, even more oddly, they can be suspicious, as if in setting a novel in a place I don't come from I've carried out some sort of fraud. Fiction may be 'made up', but it isn't fraud, and I think the 'man from the Fens' assumption betrays a very common misconception about the nature of fiction, namely, that it's really – isn't it? — some sort of disguised fact. It's the author's own experience dressed up, recycled autobiography, or it's all the result of some deliberate programme of documentary research. But if fiction is really going to be fiction, then it must involve some imaginative act, and what else is the imagination than a means of mental travel by which we can get from familiar to unfamiliar territory?

I'm thinking not just of geographical territory, but of human territory in the fullest sense. We all know that the distance between ourselves and another human being – even, sometimes, someone normally very close to us – can be immense. We often have only our imaginations to help us cross the gulf, but our imaginations can operate with remarkable speed and efficacy. Similarly, works of imaginative fiction have the ability to travel directly into a reader's mind and find a lodging there, leaping over those barriers and gaps which can normally impede the process of human contact. Without our imaginations, indeed, what isolated and confined creatures we would be. When I meet people who suppose that fiction is just a disguised form of autobiography, I'm inclined to think, well, that's their sad loss, since surely the great challenge and the great reward of fiction lies in its liberation from personal fact. The very least we should expect of it is that it should, to use the common phrase, 'take us out of ourselves', take us out of that place we normally, and sometimes narrowly, inhabit.

You don't have to have read *Waterland* to realize that my attitude to place in fiction is rather ambiguous – if not amphibious. The title itself is an invented word, suggesting not so much a single place but a place where different territories, different elements meet and become confused. If you look through my work generally, you will find quite a few edges, borderlines and borderlands of one form or another – areas of uncertain or disputed territory. I'm rather drawn to shores and the seaside. But again I'm talking not just geographically, but of all those frequently encountered mental regions where one thing can give way to another – where the present, for example, can give way to the past and to memory, history to story, the actual to the imagined, the known to the unknown. Surely we all exist most of the time in just such indeterminate territory, where the ground is always shifting under our feet. And certainly one cannot be a writer of fiction for long without starting to explore that quintessential borderline, which can never be precisely charted, between what we call, by common consent, the 'real', existing world and those worlds which are also real – since they can have real and strong effects on us – but which exist, perhaps, only in our heads. I think all fiction is continuously investigating that elusive frontier.

The Fens of my novel are to some extent imaginary, landscapes of the mind, but I hope they are also 'real' in the sense of having an authentic local texture and flavour. I'd like to stress that word 'local'. More recently, I wrote another novel called *Last Orders*, which, when it came out, might have been called my most local book, since its setting is literally close to home for me: South London and South East England. It's even written in a local language which, without attempting to be an exact transcription, reflects the language of South London. More recently still, I wrote another novel called *The Light of Day*, which could be considered even more local, since it's set in Wimbledon, which has the London postal code SW19, and I live in SW18. I was writing the novel just a long stone's throw from its location, and the logistics of my topographical research were not exactly demanding.

Wimbledon is a pretty ordinary, suburban place – places, in fact, don't come much more middling and commonplace. But the novel, I hope, explores some fairly strange and displaced worlds – the world of prison, for example, or of refugees. And in any case, I hope it explores, as I hope all my work does, the capacity within us all, even while we remain in familiar surroundings, to step into unexpected zones, to cross lines of inner geography.

You don't have to have been to Wimbledon or to the Fens to appreciate novels that may be set in those places. It's the job of the novel to take you there. I think we all recognize as readers that often rather delicious sensation, as we begin a novel, of entering a previously unfamiliar world and of starting to inhabit it as if it were our own. And we all recognize that much more intense and resonant thrill a novel can give when something in the narrative or in the internal workings of a character makes us stop in our mental tracks and say to ourselves, 'But I've been here too. I've been in this place too. It's unfamiliar, but it's not.'

It's surely this 'I've-been-here-too' territory which is the real heartland of fiction and the real destination of storytelling. It's clearly a universal territory – if we can say that we've been there too – but I think we are only truly led there by the local. The local is the route and the key to the universal, if only because it is a universal law that all experience is local and has to be placed. This is why I can happily read a novel set in some country or city I've never visited, in which a great many of the local details may, on one level, completely pass me by, but, on another level, they're not passing me by, since they're giving me that authentic, recognizable flavour of life as it's truly, locally lived.

It's the stubborn localness of our lived lives that makes the notion of a 'globalized' world, where a common currency of experience and culture is externally imposed, look dubious and spurious. We're all alike in our localness, but we don't all have to speak Esperanto, or, fortunately, write in it. Clearly, the world is becoming more 'globalized' in certain superficial ways. But, clearly, it's also becoming more dislocated. Its political and cultural boundaries are becoming ever more volatile, breachable or disputable. We would all recognize that we live in a world of increasing displacement. It might be thought that writers, who, after all, need some fixed point, some place of relative non-disturbance to do what they do, aren't well equipped to reflect such a world. But I would disagree, if only because of that central imaginative act our work involves. I think if you start a story and it's going to go anywhere, you have to engage from the outset in a sort of inner uprooting. You have to render yourself 'unattached', with all the excitement and risk that can entail.

My family's history includes at least one generation of migrants from the other side of Europe, but I would recognize that I'm a very 'indigenous' writer – practising what I do just a few miles from where I was born. On the other hand, I don't much care for putting national or geographical labels on writing: 'English writing', 'Scottish writing', 'African writing' and so on. It often seems to me to be prejudicial, restrictive and subject to needless arguments about definition. The term 'international writing' can also be bogus. Critics and reviewers in this country regularly complain that 'English' (or 'British') writers are too parochial and not 'international' enough – not, perhaps, like all those foreign writers from international places like Cuba or Egypt?

The plain words 'writing' and 'writer' are good enough for me, and any decent writer will both honour and transcend his or her locality. Wherever they hail from and whether they're like me or have actually been uprooted and displaced by life, I think all writers would acknowledge that *mental* dislocation is part and parcel of what they do. It's even what initiates and inspires what they do. All stories, I believe, are sparked off by something very simple, if potentially very complex and powerful, and to be found anywhere and everywhere: the sense of the strange. They reflect our sense of some other, mysterious world – wonderful, terrible, or just confusing, unpredictable and hard to explain – that lies close to the skin of our familiar world. *Terra incognita* can, of course, be that remote place at the edge of the map, but it can also often be just on our doorstep.

Writing Worlds 1
The Norwich Exchanges

Writing and Moral Duty

A. B. Yehoshua *Writing and Moral Value*

I have been troubled for some time, both as a writer and as a reader and teacher of literature, by questions concerning the relationship between art in general – literature, theatre and cinema, in particular – and what we tend to define as the field of morality, ethics, or moral values (terms for which I shall shortly attempt to supply more accurate definitions). It has been difficult in recent years to find in written critiques of novels, stories, plays or even films a direct reference to the moral issues raised by the work, or to the writer's good or bad moral judgment, or to the behaviour of the characters in the work. Very rarely, nowadays, are we able to hear a reader's cry of protest or wonder at the moral stance taken by a character or author in a work of literature. Even more rarely is it possible to find a reader or a critic bold enough to tie his or her protest or wonder to an aesthetic evaluation of the work. The most common words in the language of criticism, both professional and private, in evaluating a literary work are 'credibility', 'complexity', 'depth' and – especially – 'novelty'. Only very infrequently is it possible to find words such as 'moral', 'value', 'right' and 'good'.

In the second chapter of his excellent book *The Company We Keep* (1988), Wayne C. Booth bemoans how difficult it is for modern literary critics when they try to discuss the moral aspects of a work of prose. Booth's claim is that among all the various schools of thought, not one exists that dares to define itself as 'moral criticism'. Although here and there one can find moral references under various headings, the fact remains that these references must be hidden behind or annexed to discussions bearing different titles – such as 'political', 'social', 'cultural', 'psychological' or 'psychoanalytical' – or to discussions dealing with reader response, feminist commentary, or the text's discourse of power, which serves to prove the extent to which straightforward and open discussion on the moral aspects of a text has become problematic and unfashionable. Mr Booth is right to be surprised. Indeed, until the end of the 19th century, all lovers of literature expected a clear-cut regard for the moral values presented in a piece of literature and saw no reason to conceal the moral issue under such neutral terms as 'significant shape' or 'aesthetic integrity'.

Why does literary criticism, both professional and lay, withdraw from moral discussions or at least hesitate to speak out? And why has literature itself recently been blurring the natural moral conflicts that appear in the tissue of the text and pushing them backstage? I shall try to sum up several explanations that arise from Booth's book and some of my own thoughts.

The first explanation springs from the strengthening and deepening knowledge of psychology, which makes it possible to understand better the sources of failings and discrepancies in human behaviour, an understanding that causes us to reduce greatly the strength of our moral and overall judgment. To understand, ergo to forgive, so said the poet. Indeed, the more sophisticated our psychological understanding, the more difficult it is for us to connect to the simple and obvious moral judgment required of us with regard to a character such as Shakespeare's Iago, or Molière's Tartuffe or Dickens's Fagin or Pecksniff. Until the end of the 19th century, it was possible to present, whether through psychological naïvety or psychological principle, an evil and corrupt person or a pure and good person as a firm factor within the human situation described in a piece of literature. Today, it seems as though it is less easy for the serious modern novelist to present a major character whose good or bad traits are a given element that is thrown into the story without any extra explanations. In our current awareness, there is no such thing as a person who is simply bad or good. Such a person is disturbed, deprived of love, paranoid, frustrated, filled with all sorts of complexes inherited by his or her parents or surroundings. On the other hand, a pleasant and good character in a novel cannot be accepted at face value without causing us to suspect that the goodness and charity that character reflects are no more than responses to hidden and crooked impulses, whose mantle of righteousness can be pulled aside to allow them to cause damage to their environment.

Meursault, hero of Camus's *The Stranger* (a novella of such importance that I believe it opened the era of modern literature following the Second World War), who, for no reason, shoots an Arab on the beach in Algeria, cannot be seen as a bad person according to the new concept. He is 'alienated' or 'shallow'; he does not understand the ways of the world. It is modernism that is guilty of his crime. In other cases, novelists will rake up childhood hardships in order to understand the moral misformations on the soul. Society, economic conditions, parent-child relations are placed on trial as powerful partners to the character's evil deeds.

In his novel *Crime and Punishment*, Dostoyevsky omitted many details about Raskolnikov's childhood, made little of his having lost his father as a child, and did not develop a real elaboration on his relationship with his mother and sister. He made these choices, I believe, so that psychology (Dostoyevsky had a deep knowledge and sensitive attitude to psychology) would not attract our attention from the moral dilemma that stands at the novel's centre: does an individual have the right for self-fulfilment via the murder of a 'human flea'? A murder of this kind is no longer possible in a modern-day novel because psychology would not let him remain within the simplicity of his own moral dilemma. Other murderers in Dostoyevsky's later novels, such as Rogozhin in *The Idiot* and Smerdyakov in *The Brothers Karamazov*, are wrapped in a psychological blanket that is stronger than Raskolnikov's. Of course, I do not think that in the end the psychological explanations dispel all the moral dilemmas awakened by the text, but they do dull the immediate sharpness of these dilemmas and force us to hone and vary our definitions of moral judgment to those areas covered by psychology.

The second reason for the withdrawal of moral judgment from literary criticism springs from the growth of legal influence in our lives, which is gradually overshadowing moral debate. More and more we tend to see the world through legal rather than ethical spectacles. Because we live in a democratic society, in which we are supposed to have faith in our system of law-making, we are used to the fact that the place in which to settle disputes regarding good or bad is the courthouse, where sharp-tongued lawyers are able sometimes to prove that a murderer is not exactly a murderer, but something else. We identify what is good in accordance with what the law allows us and what is bad in accordance with what the law forbids us. If we are allowed to drive at 100 miles per hour, it must be good, even if it creates a clear danger to human life. Sexual harassment is what the law defines as sexual harassment, which frees us from the need to take a personal stance that defines the act as good or bad and leaves the decision to the law. And because we feel that the legal system is constantly increasing its boundaries and becoming more liberal and advanced, we are quite content to let it do our moral work for us.

The third reason, I believe, is tied to the amazing development over recent years of the media in all its aspects, which also deals – admittedly on a superficial level – with moral issues, but also with speed, efficiency and perseverance, both on social and personal levels. Literature often seems to be preceded by the media in penetrating certain new moral issues – for example those concerning medicine or the status of women or homosexuality – because the media has a way of connecting quickly and immediately to the demands of political correctness, which is basically led by moral sensitivities that demand more equality between various sectors of society and atonement for old injustices. The widespread exposure enjoyed by the media makes its moral work both popular and immediate, and it seems to literature that nothing is left but to save its honour and hide away in its own little neurotic corner and try to pluck out yet another undiscovered psychological nuance or two – or to bemoan the superficiality of modern life. Indeed, there is something ironic about the fact that in keeping with the demands of political correctness, current literary editors (especially American ones) diligently weed out the 'moral ineptitude' and the literary slips of the tongue that spring from the shortage of sensitivity and that are sprinkled liberally in modern short stories and novels. In other words, not only is it of no use to expect the writers to lead and invent the new sensitivities, but it is necessary to check them and make sure they do not stumble over the 'mistakes' of the past.

The fourth reason is based on the fear that any moral discussion, especially during our own century, with its clear and definite ideological character, might sneak in a kind of ideological censorship – whether religious or otherwise – that would take the side either of the writer or the reader. Such censorship would occur not necessarily in countries under totalitarian communist or fascist government, but in countries that enjoy democratic freedom of the kind that is constantly subjected to stormy ideological debates such as the one surrounding socialism.

Anyway – and this allegation might be the harshest against moral discussion in literature – can there be objective criteria according to which a serious debate can be conducted on this issue at this of all times, when literary criticism is doing its best to adopt clear and accurate tools for research? After all, what a writer sees as moral or immoral – or even amoral – in this or that behaviour of the characters he or she created is not necessarily obvious to his or her readers. It is especially difficult to reach a consensus among readers on one or other moral judgment when we tend more and more to assume (and respect) the multiplicity of cultural – and moral – codes in human society.

When literary criticism involves itself with the analysis of philology or the form and structure of a text or even the psychological motives of the characters, it appeals first and foremost to the reader's comprehension and relies on an understanding resulting from a mutual reading of the text. But the moment it begins dealing with moral evaluation, it finds itself entering the scope of extremely relative issues that must take into consideration all the various moral shades in each individual reader's stance because a moral stance is, in the final analysis, a personal stance. And because these various fine shades are what interest us in a literary text, an agreed upon, accepted debate and certainly any moral judgment and evaluation become difficult and complex.

I have only one reply to all these assertions, which is, to me at least, also quite convincing: whether we like it or not, every artistic work that deals with human relations has in it a moral aspect because all human relationships may be evaluated according to moral categories.

The existence of a moral aspect in every piece of prose is what caused Jean-Paul Sartre to define the essential difference between prose (and in this case, theatre also) and the other arts (including poetry) in his well-known book *What is Literature?* In all the other arts, no significant regard is given to issues of morality in the form and artistic context of a work, whereas in prose, theatre, and cinema there exists a moral regard in the mere fact of presenting the relationships between characters.

Morality is not some far-off shining star suspended in the sky of our lives. It is omnipresent, it can be found everywhere that human beings are conducting interpersonal relationships, from the small cell that constitutes a marriage or family, to an individual's society, to his or her nation, and even to the international community. It may be that the commentator on a certain work of literature will find that its author or one of his or her heroes makes no reference whatsoever to questions of ethics that are demanded by certain situations. The reader, however, is entitled to relate to this lack and to try to learn from it about the quality and intentions of the novel's heroes. Even the black holes left behind by the novel, those things that remain unsaid and undone, are an integral part of it, and their effect on the reading is part of the creative activity.

The withdrawal of literature from the scope of large-scale moral debate is not good either for literature or for morality because no matter how professionally successful the work of the media and the importance of the courts of law, they are not as capable of bringing a person to so deep a level of empathy as is literature. Supposing, for example, that instead of the wonderful book by Harriet Beecher Stowe, *Uncle Tom's Cabin* (which was published in 1852 and aroused such deep and active empathy among people in the northern United States, that it turned into a powerful myth throughout the country and prompted so many to join the struggle for the abolition of slavery), a TV crew had been sent to *Uncle Tom's Cabin* to interview the slave and, to maintain a balance, his owners as well. I doubt if, under such circumstances, the spiritual and perhaps political results would have been the same.

There is a significant difference between the way in which literature creates the moral catharsis and the activity of the media. Literature does not expect its devotees to understand, but to identify. The power of this identification lies in the fact that the moral issue does not remain on the cognitive level, but becomes part of the reader's personality and independence, his or her own personal problem. Thus, the moral touch, if it succeeds, shocks the deeper strata of the individual's soul.

Plato feared the effect of the negative morality of poets and believed that they and their poetry had to be checked very carefully before being given a place in his ideal state. In his old age, Tolstoy spoke out against a certain kind of literature, including his own great novels, because he was concerned about their amoral effect on society. The two shared a common belief that art, especially literature, has a powerful spiritual influence and a clear moral affinity. Nowadays, such theories would be received with a smile of derision. Nowadays, the attitude to art and literature is not so serious and concerned, and no such heavy responsibility is heaped upon them.

About seventy years ago in a Paris concert hall, an angry audience threw rotten eggs at the performers of Stravinsky's ballet *The Rite of Spring* because they saw in this music a coarse provocation against all their values, not only musical but also moral. Who would take the trouble today of protesting in the name of values of any kind – even uttering a polite cry – against a modernistic piece of music or a new book? At most, there would be lack of interest, a shrug of the shoulder, or weak applause, a fear that this composition might in time turn out to be a new version of *The Rite of Spring*. In the world of entertainment, everything goes, and the only question is whether it was a success or not. That is why no one expects literature to deliver any 'new tidings', rather merely an 'experience'.

Edited extracts from the introduction to The Terrible Power of a Minor Guilt: Literary Essays *by A.B. Yehoshua, translated from the Hebrew by Ora Cummings, Syracuse: Syracuse University Press, 2000. Reprinted here with the kind permission of the author.*

In conversation: Gillian Beer, Christopher Bigsby, Tessa de Loo and George Szirtes

Gillian Beer:

There were several things that I partly agreed with in what A.B. Yehoshua had to say, for example, his emphasis on identification. One of the things that I felt got left out is the degree to which the reader is always in a state of resistance to what he or she reads.

There are two things that are contradictory. One is that the reader never reads entirely in his or her own person; the reader is made by the book they are reading. The second is that the reader is not sitting there, thoroughly prepared for the work. Behind the work, there are already some common assumptions and expectations which are being drawn on by the reader as well.

What I did find very surprising was the emphasis on the absence of such concerns in current writing. If one turns to something like J.M. Coetzee's *Disgrace*, which starts with sexual harassment and moves through to a grim exploration of the degree of each person's responsibility for his or her actions and for what happens to them, one can move through Coetzee's writing career to *Elizabeth Costello* which is concerned with the rights of animals and the degree to which humans have become over-preoccupied with human concerns. This is a work of the most profound moral order; a very uncomfortable work to read, and a very disagreeable work in some ways. Or, if we turn, of course, to Toni Morrison, surely in her writing we find precisely those profound human concerns and a willingness to name evil. All the while, as you were arguing, there is a deep concern with complexity and psychology, the disturbed and the paranoid, a willingness to know that all this disturbance produces results which are evil because they undermine and devalue other people. Or, one could take Les Murray's *Translations from the Natural World* which gives a voice to the trouble of translating from the animal to the human. This seems to me to be one of the preoccupations that is so strong in the most concerned writing. What Murray does is to break, to plot, to manipulate human language in such a way that we realize these are translations. They are not smoothing out the difference between human and animal, they are letting us see that the voice has come from a place we can't quite share.

I wouldn't be willing to accept that there is no such declarative force in current literature. You started by saying that the reader's cry of protest is rarely heard. These are all writers who provoke in us cries of protest, make us feel that we can't quite live in the world conjured, that we are going to have to relearn, to be another person in order to inhabit such a world thoroughly and securely.

That seems to me to be one of the miracles of what literature can do.

In the first half you were saying that there once were all these great writers and now – where are they? It's always very difficult to recognize the great writers when you are close to them.

There's a lovely glassworks in Cambridge, which has been there for about 150 years called Constable. Up on the wall there is a great sign that has been there for 100 years or so, that runs like this:

> Curved is the line of beauty
> Straight is the line of duty
> Follow the straight line
> Thou shalt see the curved line ever follow thee.

If only things were so simple. When I was reading Alan Hollinghurst's *The Line of Beauty* I found myself haunted by this sign, which is different in its formulation but not entirely different in its moral bearings from what Hollinghurst is doing. The question is: is beauty enough? I don't see pleasure as separate from moral force. Pleasure seems to me to be the initiating form of moral force, allowing us to enter these profound questions.

George Szirtes:

The act of writing is a moral act in that one is endeavouring to come at some profound human truth. You value a work of art; its morality is embedded in its search for this profound human truth. Its subject may not necessarily be a particular moral conflict but the conflict is embedded within the work. The pleasure is not of the order of a nice ice cream or a good meal or anything like that; it is a profound pleasure of being aware that these deep human truths exist and may be embodied in a flimsy thing like a book.

Tessa de Loo:

When it comes to morality in literature, the role of the critic is also important. In Holland some of the most influential critics perhaps give too much praise for a kind of nihilism in literature – a phenomenon that started, as A.B. Yehoshua just said, with Camus's *L'Etranger.* Nihilistic novels suggest that the reader should not identify with the protagonist but rather be shocked, because the protagonist reflects our modern society, where traditional morality seems to be increasingly lacking. More than 50 years later the intellectual admiration for nihilism might create a distance between the common reader, always searching for a deeper moral order, and literature.

Christopher Bigsby:

I've been a little bit surprised. There is usually a tendency for morality to be talked about as if it is a sweet inside a wrapping paper, whereas we are talking about morality inherent in the fiction maker's occupation. Writing is a quintessentially moral act, which is partly why we describe things as humanities.

Talking about the value of a work of art can lead to many debates. Despite the difficulties with Kant's discussion of artistic value I agree with him that this is partly determined by the pleasure we derive from it. This pleasure is neither moral nor sensual. Kant distinguishes between three kinds of pleasure: a pleasure we achieve through doing the right thing – moral pleasure; a pleasure of eating and having sex – sensual pleasure; and the aesthetic pleasure. Aesthetic pleasure, Kant argues, unlike the other kinds of pleasures, is totally disinterested. By this he means that we do not enjoy a work of art to satisfy any end within us, be it moral or sensual, but we enjoy it as an end in itself.

I believe it's too ambitious to talk about aesthetic value in general, because the kind of pleasure derived from listening to a piece of music is different from looking at a painting or reading a novel. Here I concentrate on literary value, and when I say a work of art I mean a work of literature. If we apply Kant's theory to literature, we will have to argue that for a piece of writing to be valuable, it has to please us not because it's a moral or sexually exciting piece of work, but because we can take disinterested pleasure in it.

What exactly is this disinterested pleasure? Kant argues that a poem, for example, is valuable because it carries an aesthetic idea, which is expressed in a way that quickens our senses. When we read a good work of art, all our mental faculties, by which he means the imagination and the understanding, are in harmony and perfection with each other. In this sense, a valuable work of art has the capacity to make us feel more complete. This does not mean that a work of art cannot disturb or puzzle us, but in doing so, it brings our mental faculties to a sort of togetherness, which may explain why we derive pleasure from tragedy.

Mourid Barghouti talked about how the notion of shared spaces is threatened more than ever. When he mentioned that 69 Palestinian women gave birth at checkpoints and the children so-born grew up in restricted space, their path to school forever divided by checkpoints, the notion of place is far from the ordinary. A.B. Yehoshua argued that Mourid's story does not deal with the complexity of the situation, and therefore is not fair. The story talks about women giving birth at checkpoints but does not mention why the checkpoints exist. A.B. Yehoshua talked about the issue of morality in judging a work of art and how we cannot ignore the moral aspect in works of literature. Our discussion showed that for many writers the morality of a work of art does enter into consideration.

I have divided feelings about this. On the one hand, whether a work of literature is moral or not, it can be good or bad. If we decide to cleanse the literary scene by erasing literature that has racist, colonialist or orientalist aspects, we may have to demolish many great works of literature. On the other hand, I am aware of the power of literature to re-emphasize negative stereotypes and to justify the imbalanced power relationships in the world. Maybe the best thing is to be aware of the moral dimension of the work without having to abandon it altogether. Gillian Beer pointed to the reader's resistance, which I think is a key concept in this debate. But this requires a mature, aware and intelligent reader. I read *Gone With The Wind* when I was 15 and living in Iran. All I saw in it was a love story. It was only when I was 21 and in the UK that I realized the racial dimension in the novel.

Eva Hoffman pointed out that maybe we should use the word 'seriousness' instead of 'morality'. By this she meant that a work of literature should expand our humanness, and that its value lies in how seriously it attempts to do so. This resonates with George Szirtes's comment that good literature aims at the truth, and refined pleasure lies in becoming aware that these human truths exist.

In this sense, thinking clearly and writing clearly are essential in order to reclaim language and abide by the truth. Then comes the question: whose truth? But I hope that the readers' intelligence and resistance will help them judge the work. The truth is not always a black and white matter; there are many times, listening to an argument, that we understand and sympathize with both sides. This may be a truth in itself – to be forever open, to be curious and prepared for a work of art to unsettle us. I believe that as readers and writers, we are forever concerned with truth and justice. I write to define the blind spots of truth and justice that exist in all of us. I write to challenge norms, challenge the people who decide whose cause is justified and whose is not, whose voice will be heard and whose will be silent, whose suffering is more important. I write to tell my truth, the one that has been ignored, sidelined and silenced. Only when we know the whole truth can we try to make the right decision and act in the right way.

Writing Worlds 1
The Norwich Exchanges

Writing, Language, Translation

I heard of a man who took his small daughter on a visit to the House of Lords. After some while watching in silence while one of our many unelected representatives in all his regalia held forth, the little girl asked in quite a loud voice, 'What's that man for, Daddy?' Since I translate a lot of poetry, and with my wife co-edit *Modern Poetry in Translation*, I suppose I ought to be able to say what translators are for, what good they are, what use. But also, since my chief concern as a writer is poetry, I must try to say what poets are for. Or better: what *good* poetic language is.

Writing poetry and translating it are, for me, intimately connected undertakings. By no means identical, they are nonetheless closely analogous; and much of what I might say about the one, I could say about the other.

Uses of Translation

Relations between languages, nations and cultures alter continually, under the influence of very many different forces. But most, perhaps all, of these forces might be roughly flung together under one heading: relative power. The relative power of cultures determines not only what each might import from another but also *how*, in what ways and to what purpose.

During the Thirty Years War, for example, Germany's language and culture seemed to be heading towards extinction under the armies of many nations criss-crossing the land. Yet in that desperate context a literature was created; or we might say, invented. And how? By the main force of translation. Most of the credit must go to one person, Martin Opitz, known in his day as the Prince of German Poets. Almost single-handedly he assembled at least the building blocks of a national literature. Translating (more or less directly) from French, Dutch, Italian, English, Latin and Greek, he provided examples, where there had been none, in all three genres – lyric, epic, dramatic – for his successors (writers and translators) to imitate and excel. German literature of the 17th century derives its very existence from Seneca's drama, Ronsard's sonnets, English and Italian pastoral, the Spanish picaresque novel....

Translation was the maker of a literature. And it was so again, though to a lesser degree, around 1760 because of large imports from France and England, which would then be adapted or violently opposed by the great and very German writers of the *Goethezeit*. And there was another beginning in 1945, after 12 years of prohibition under Hitler, when foreign literatures were allowed back in. Imported short stories, for example, in distinctively American and British forms, gave young writers like Heinrich Böll models for a new starting point in his country's catastrophe. Germany's literary tradition is a thing of fits and starts. It is, relatively speaking, an unconfident tradition, often dislocated, lapsing into anxiety about itself, looking abroad for new impulses.

Britain's literary dealings with abroad, with the neighbouring and the distant nations, their living and their so-called dead languages, have been more self-confident, but vastly beneficial to Britain all the same. Translation into English is more than a bit like immigration into Britain. We – our literature, our culture – are unimaginable without it. We imported French and Italian romances, Spanish novels, Greek and Latin myths, history and biography – large forms, techniques, materials, sensibilities. But also quite particular poetic shapes; the sonnet, for example, introduced by Wyatt and Surrey from Petrarch in the 16th century, still practised, endlessly varying, today. Blank verse, the unrhyming iambic pentameter, was invented by Surrey, for his translation of the *Aeneid*. He wanted a line as adaptable and resonant as the Latin hexameter. Brought in by translation for that specific purpose, blank verse very soon established itself as the English language's chief poetic and dramatic line. And because of its closeness to the natural rhythms of English speech and because, without forfeiting its identity, it can be handled and can sound very differently, it lives and thrives still today. Translation, as an importer of foreign goods or as a deviser of equivalent forms, has been a powerful shaper of English literature.

Britain today, out of timidity, laziness, complacency, insularity and frank xenophobia, is far less open to foreign literatures than it ought to be. Only about three percent of total literary publication in Britain is translation, and only about 25% of that 3% is translated poetry.

Modern Poetry in Translation was founded by Ted Hughes and Daniel Weissbort in 1965. They had two important aims, which they combined into one: to get writers like Herbert, Milosz, Holub and Lalić out from behind the Iron Curtain into a wider readership in English; and to benefit British poetry by so doing. Translation allied itself with foreign and native poetry in a vital undertaking. The Soviet bloc needed to export. Britain needed to import. We need such alliances and border crossings even more today.

Friedrich Hölderlin, the foreign poet I have had the closest dealings with, was a great, and eccentric, translator. In a letter to Casimir Böhlendorff, a notably wandering friend of his, he offered these profound insights into the importance of translation in the whole poetic undertaking. First, that 'what is peculiarly our own has to be learned just as much and just as well as what is foreign to us'. And second, developing the first statement, that the aim of all literal and figurative journeying abroad is to come into 'the free use of one's own'. He had in mind, and we may say that he practised in his life, the image of a journeyman who goes abroad, lives abroad and steeps himself in the foreign, knowing all the while that he will come home and enliven his native culture by bringing foreignness into it. More particularly, he will shape and understand his own language thus, by a passage through the foreign. We come into our own by going abroad.

The Foreignness of Poetic Language

There's an old question among translators which I never ask myself. Should one domesticate the foreign text into something that is, so to speak, comfortably at home in the host language? Or rather should one point up its foreignness, so that the reader is continually made aware that this is a text coming from abroad? I don't ask myself that question because the language of poetry, which I am trying to write when I translate a foreign poet, is itself always a foreign language. Robert Graves called the poet 'an ambassador of Otherwhere'. The language of that country is 'Otherwhereish'. It lives at an odd angle to any of the native language's usual vernaculars and from there works estrangingly and unsettlingly. A good translation will work similarly. Foreignness, so understood, is a vital agent in a translated poem and in a poem conceived and executed in the mother tongue. The foreignness helps to defamiliarize and unsettle.

Why wish to estrange and unsettle? To combat fundamentalism

and complacency. Every national culture needs continually to be relativized by importing foreignness and by being viewed from unfamiliar perspectives. Poetry and translation can help in that. We are, quite simply, doomed unless we allow ourselves to be shown that the way things are is not the way they have to be. The estrangement of our systems and beliefs, their being set alongside other possibilities, should, at the very least, make us sceptical of all absolutes. Translation and poetry, forever bringing in Otherness, are powerful solvents and un-doers of all absolute claims.

Liveliness

English, particularly American English, marches over the globe, but it spreads itself very thinly in doing so. As Eurospeak or the worldwide *lingua franca*, English is becoming a merely serviceable thing. Translation is close reading, perhaps the closest reading; and translators, reading thus, know how unique each language is, and how irreducible and intractable (and untranslatable) is its incarnate spirit. But that spirit is sold away when a language is reduced to the condition of being merely serviceable. Poets and translators have a duty to make their languages resistant to such reduction and enslavement.

It is a sad fact, and all translators know it, that the original work lives on and on while most translations, even the very good ones, die within a generation. Why don't translations last like the originals? The answer, saying everything and nothing, is that original works have more vitality. Vital in themselves and in the liveliness of their language, they become vital to us, we cannot do without them, and we keep them alive in every generation by re-reading them, and in that way figuratively, and then often literally, re-translating them. We translate them into the most living language we can, the liveliest at our disposal. Or we should always strive to. But it has been statistically proven that in syntax, vocabulary, idiom, tone and texture, most translations are less various than their foreign originals. Some translators allow themselves to be pulled towards a consensus speech, something that will not offend or be too difficult. In translating novels for a British and American market they may even be instructed to avoid anything either readership might think peculiar. But mid-Atlantic language is no language at all. It will have largely forfeited its vital power, becoming merely serviceable, conveying a plot. Vital originals do not occupy the middle ground (far less the mid-ocean); they live and work in their peculiarity. Translators need to bear that in mind and resist the pull towards the middle and the consensus.

We want a lively language. We want a language that will quicken people into a sense of other possibilities. Eliot spoke of purifying 'the dialect of the tribe', but that is the last thing we want. We want to enliven our tribal tongues by bringing in the foreign, to provoke what Lawrence called 'a new effort of attention'. In fact, to effect a shift of consciousness.

The Free Use of One's Own

Hölderlin came fully into his own poetic language by translating Pindar word for word. Against the foreign language he understood better what his mother tongue could be made to do. Poets who translate have an eye on the health and vigour of their own language even as they attend minutely to the demands of the foreign. When I translate, I learn. I watch how German grammar and syntax work to the advantage of the German poem, and ask myself continually what of those workings might be transferred into my English, for similar, analogous or quite different (and estranging) effects. For example, German grammar sends the verb and its auxiliaries to the end of a subordinate clause. The reading mind has to wait for sense to be completed. This deferral may be quite lengthy. I like that extending hesitancy. It seems to me good that when we read we should not close down too soon. Such syntax, normal and correct in German, can be managed so that options are held open for quite some time. And an English writer who thinks this a valuable effect can seek for ways either usual or not unbearably unusual in English which could engender it.

There *is* virtue, I think, in delaying the moment when the reading mind settles into certainty; even in hindering that certainty altogether. The brain is programmed in the expectation of the familiar, its responses are ready and waiting. Poetry disconcerts it, makes it try again. This has to be managed delicately, of course. Bafflement is not productive. Rather, there should be a continual delicate teasing, a thwarting of stock responses, a quickening to other possibilities.

I'm speaking here (alas, without the time to demonstrate the practice in examples) about effects which are proven and readily intelligible. All poems achieve them more or less abundantly, and translators, observing them in one language, will seek to carry them across into the other. And I am giving these effects a moral colouring, calling them valuable, saying there is virtue in them. I make no apology for that. When I write and translate poems, I do indeed believe the poetic line – enlivening, unsettling and defamilarizing – to be a force for good. A reader enjoying and alerted by the syntax and rhythms of poetry, disposed by the workings of poetic lines to entertain a variety of possibilities, will, I believe, in his or her life as a citizen, be better able to answer back.

Answering Back

Poetry shares its medium – words – with many forms of speech and writing that are quite unlike it; indeed, with several towards which it must remain implacably hostile. Poetry has to contend with – I mean, compete with and struggle against – a great deal of *bad language.*

By bad language I don't just mean the public foul-mouthedness that, in Britain at least, has become so prevalent we seem intended by some Authority to have to get used to it. I don't just mean that, though its effects – a coarsening of the feelings and a reduction of the power of speech – are certainly very harmful. I mean chiefly the many official speakers and writers who cannot or will not say what they mean. The purveyors of gobbledygook, evasions and lies.

There is some gobbledygook in the universities. Because of an acquiescence to false models, there is nowadays much management-speak. But in a university, which is a community of people teaching and learning, we have a right to expect clarity, truth, plain speaking; language used to proper point and purpose, truly to instruct, to edify, to excite, inspire, warn, alert and rouse. Instead, you may well get this:

> All components of summative assessment should be included
> as a percentage contribution to the total assessment.
> This is vital in monitoring the assessment/credit weighting
> relationship and student workload. If the learning outcomes

describe a student centred learning approach with a group-based approach but the assessment is predominantly unseen exams, an incompatibility will be detected.

We simply can't afford to accustom people to language like that.

But worse, much worse, is the language of the torturers. Two recent publications, *The Torture Papers* and *Torture and Truth*, both having to do with America's War on Terror and in particular the malpractice in Abu Ghraib prison, are a thesaurus of bad language. The language was produced by lawyers asked to define torture in such a way that the nation's agents would feel free to practise it. So sleep deprivation was described as 'probably within the lexicon'. That meant 'you will probably get away with it', but to be on the safe side, call it 'sleep adjustment'. And call beatings 'enhanced interrogation techniques'. Call the people you are torturing 'sources'. Call those you think particularly well worth torturing 'high-value detainees'. Call the whole business 'prisoner-guard interactions'. Our own people in Whitehall, senior officials, acknowledged early in 2002 that they had heard: 'anecdotal reports ... of "undue exuberance" by American personnel at Guantánamo Bay'. Adjective and noun there are equally remarkable.

I don't honestly know what such language is doing, or what its users think they are doing. In fact everyone knows what 'collateral damage', 'waterboarding' and 'extraordinary rendition' mean. If they were ever intended as euphemisms, their shelf-life as such is very short. They cannot be serious efforts to hide any truth. Are they a help and a comfort to the people doing the deeds they stand for? Is a man who uses the word 'lethality' or who speaks of 'terminating with extreme prejudice', thereby enabled to kill? Are his fellow-countrymen, his friends and family, thereby enabled to live with it? Doubtful. The language, appalling and risible in equal measure, rather seems part of the deed, its ugliness, its transparent hypocrisy, its cynicism or criminal ignorance and naïvety. God struggling to keep up with us, there must by now be a circle of hell in which people will mouth such things for ever.

The statement claiming responsibility for the bombs in London on 7 July opened thus: 'In the name of God, the merciful, the compassionate, may peace be upon the cheerful one and undaunted fighter, Prophet

Mohammed, God's peace be upon him …'

This notice hangs on the wire of Camp Delta, Guantánamo Bay: 'Honor Bound to Defend Freedom.'

No doubt in both cases the writers meant what they wrote.

Of course, the deed is worse than the name. Still, it is not frivolous to wish that words should accord with and not, for whatever reason, deny or conceal, the bad deeds they are attached to. Let us say what the deed really is, then see if it is still so readily able to be done. Language is involved in our acts, good or bad; easily becomes complicit in wrongdoing, aids and abets it. Easily, whether the speaker or writer knows this or not, language becomes an agent of oppression. And if we don't watch our language, we shall be weakened and reduced in our ability to answer back. That is why it is so important that our schools and universities teach and practise the art of speaking and writing clearly. We have to be able to argue.

Conclusion

Poetic language is not itself the language in which to argue and answer back. Vigorous clear prose will do that. Poetic language is rather an intrinsic answering back. For one thing, it is beautiful and bad language is very ugly. For another, it seeks to tell the truth, and often succeeds. Poetry truly does say what things are like. Either because they cannot or because they will not, our managers, bureaucrats, politicians and their lawyers almost never say what things are truly like. Poetry, never to become the language of office, never to issue statements, is an intrinsic running metaphor for the better, the best speech, we are capable of. And by 'we' I mean not just poets, but readers; the readers who, like poets, are always also citizens.

'Translation' (like 'metaphor') means 'carrying over'. Translators carry over all they can of meaning out of one language into another. The figurative sense of that practical exercise is vast and heartening. Translation is one human activity that continually lives up to its beneficent figurative sense. Across all the frontiers of time and space, translators circulate the living word.

Returning to the anecdote I began with: that is what I think translators and poets (poetic language) are *for*.

The Language Question

In conversation: Leila Ahmed, Mourid Barghouti, Christopher Bigsby, Austin Clarke, David Constantine, Jon Cook, Alison Croggon, Vesna Goldsworthy, Choman Hardi, Eva Hoffman, Ogaga Ifowodo, Hasso Krull, David Solway, Luisa Valenzuela and Mary Woronov.

Jon Cook:

The language question was introduced to us by Eva Hoffman when she talked about moving from one language to another, from Polish to English. It has also surfaced in our discussions about living in a culture, and perhaps a literary culture, which is dominated by one language: English.

The only analogy for such domination that I can immediately think of is French during the 18th century. Latin would be an earlier equivalent. One of the things that the question about the dominance of English raises is in turn a question of translation; of being translated into English as a necessary part of gaining a certain international reputation.

We may be living in a world where a book or a collection of poetry can take on a curious kind of double life: the life that it leads in its original language and the life that it leads in its translated language. Of course, this raises many questions about what is entailed by the act of translation, both linguistically, in literary terms and culturally.

Writers can be translated, as well as their works. One of the things we discussed yesterday was the power of labels. The way in which writers, tendencies or genres get a label attached to them – perhaps as a marketing device, perhaps just as a way of fixing them in one place.

Luisa Valenzuela:

I'm not a translator myself, but I belive all writers are in some way translators. After all, the noun comes from the Latin *translatare*, that is to say to transport, to transfer, to take elsewhere. Which is what writers do, we put into words but at the same time take elsewhere our limited experience of so called 'reality', a word Nabokov always insisted should be written between quotation marks.

On the other hand, having lived in New York for over 10 years and having had my work translated there by various pros, I am aware of the different approaches to this difficult task. David said something wonderful about poetic language and how the strangeness has to be carried over from the other language, which is the craft of translators as artists, as poets in their own capacity. But it is a rare fortune to find one such artist, especially if you are a novelist. And a Latin American novelist to top it all. In which case we may stumble either upon a banalized view or an overly repectful view of the work. That is to say, a superficial or a literal reading. There is a difficult balance to achieve, and there are important choices the translator has to make. As David said, translators must respect the syntax of the original. And syntax means another way of seeing the world, practically another cosmogony.

Yesterday, we spoke about magic realism and Latin American literature. Many Anglo translators and the English-speaking public in general focus more on the 'magic' aspect, whereas we focus on the real. For us, magic realism is a more expanded way of seeing reality. It offends me when most Latin American literature is labelled as surrealist. It is an oversimplification. Surrealism may play with any idea, juggle and substitute on word for another. Latin American writers tend to be very precise and rational, albeit playing with language, making the best of multiple connotations.

Another subject raised here was the *use* of telling stories. I remember George Steiner's phrase: 'God created man so that man could tell Him stories'. Also we know – and Jerome Bruner has studied this in depth – that our understanding of the world is affected by the way we tell ourselves stories. And we do that constantly in our minds. It is not only a question of the written work. Stories are our form of understanding of the world, of accessing knowledge. Thus, it is crucial that we have access to all kind of books in translation so we may focus our understanding through different lenses. In *Border Writing: the Multidimensional Text*, Emily Hicks deals chiefly with some Latin American writers who usually work with two sets of codes. She coined the term 'cultural smuggler'. We smuggle from one way of seeing the world to another.

When David talked about how English has become the *lingua franca*, the internet came to mind, for English has taken over the cyberspace. That so very English letter, 'w', is tripled: we have 'www', where things seem to become monolithic and monolingual. This can work against your so rich language, English, in the sense of narrowing the vocabulary.

But what really worries me is the fact that we have entered the third millennium, yet everything looks exactly the same as it did last century; the dresses and vehicles and houses, all. The visible has not changed. But the invisible is all pervasive and even threatening. What cell phones can do today, just to put one example, we couldn't even have imagined some years ago. There is also the internet, the human genome, the cloning business. All these impressive discoveries are invisible, but they are modifying our lives. How can we translate or transmit all these changes when we are still writing as we used to write in the last century?

Heidegger's 'house of language' is now hidden under scaffolding, *Sloterdijk dixit*, and we don't know what will happen when the scaffolding is removed. This is why I was thinking that writers do not so much inhabit the house of language as are inhabited by language. We are prisoners of language but we are also its guardians. I'm thinking of what David said about the dangerous metaphors and euphemisms that are being used against humanity. The Argentine use of the term 'disappeared', adopted by the military to name those who had been badly tortured and killed, so as to erase them not only from the face of the earth but even from memory. Perhaps translation is a way of not allowing such disappearances to take place.

I come from a country where, being a third world country, we read lots of works in translation. We had all of the best books in the world translated into Spanish. I can vouch for the importance of knowing everybody else's cultures as much as our own.

David Solway:

I'm a little bit taken aback. I feel very nervous; it's probably quite visible although usually I can fake confidence well. I feel very nervous because I want to say something that I'm sure almost everybody in the room will not agree with or will find in some way offensive. And I'm also nervous because what I want to say is also perhaps mischievous; it comes in from a different angle.

Let me start briefly with a short anecdote. Not long ago I attended a conference in Montreal featuring five intellectuals of very high standing: three from Quebec, one from Belgium, one from France. The man who spoke, the man from Paris, who was speaking about the relation between culture and language, began his deposition by saying, 'I see a direct line between Cro-Magnon and George Bush.' This had nothing to do with the deposition he was about to make but at that moment he had the entire audience with him because Francophile Montreal is entirely anti-American, anti the war on Iraq, anti what happened in Afghanistan. So immediately there was a kind of political shoehorn into a cultural discussion. He had the audience with him.

A short time after that I heard a speech by Carlos Fuentes, who I think is a great writer, one of my favourite writers. He began by speaking in three languages. He began by saying, 'We, down south of the border, and you, north of the border, we are united by the country that divides us.' Immediately he had the audience with him. The United States is the great enemy, the great Satan, not only amongst the people of the East or the Islamic peoples, but also among the left-wing intellectuals of which I was one until about two years ago. Immediately you have a kind of collaborative audience with whom you do not have to worry, to defend yourself. They will be with you no matter what you say. Now here's the point I want to make:

Everything you said about translation, I endorse, you are perfectly right. It was a brilliant talk, David. What I object to is your selection of examples. For instance, when you speak about torture, introducing the notion of torture-speak or double-speak, your examples, your illustrations were apt but they were also one-sided. After 9/11, in the last couple of years, I've discussed these issues with some of my Islamic friends. My video provider in the little town of Hudson is Iranian, and when I asked him about 9/11 he said, 'We must cleanse the world of evil.' That was his form of torture-speak, or double-speak. Peter Dale Scott, whom some of you might know, was a Canadian poet, the son of Frank Scott, one of our forefathers in Canadian poetry. Peter Dale Scott went south of the border; he was teaching at Berkeley for a while. After 9/11, when he was introduced to a class, he would say, 'What we call an act of terror is really an act of courage. To ride the aeroplanes in; that takes courage.' And he had the whole class with him, but we know where Berkeley is.

Now, when you speak about pulling fingernails, about CIA talk, I couldn't agree more, I think that's horrific. When you choose illustrations or examples from a certain perspective you are also committing, in a sense, a form of special pleading, you're using a concessionary rhetoric. The choice of your examples may also be a form of double-speak. It accedes to that which it wants to do away with and therefore, it is a kind of false translation. What I'm saying is, why not introduce examples from both sides so that the idea becomes not simply a political idea, but is expressing a variety of conceptions; not simply a selection of examples that corresponds to one particular form of diction. It is not just a question of the language that you use or how you use the language or how you evade reality, it's a question of the examples that you decide to select in order to evade another kind of reality.

David Constantine:

I quoted a man from Whitehall talking about 'undue exuberance.' Had I had the time, I could have shown you a sheaf of papers from a British university, to illustrate the language of bureaucracy. I might have qouted our Prime Minister and out Attorney General in their wonderfully evasive utterances on the subject of Guantánamo Bay.

It is not possible to be exhaustive in twenty minutes, and I tried to keep the question of truth. I actually put it to you: I do not know what they mean by language like that. I'm honestly at a loss to understand the strategies. Perhaps I didn't connect it well enough. What I should have said more fully is that I do indeed view the language of poetry, when properly handled, as a way of answering back against all kinds of language that do not seek to tell the truth.

The premise in all my literary undertakings is that I am trying to tell the truth. An awful lot of people are manifestly not using language as a means of telling the truth. I offered some examples.

Mary Woronov:

Your examples were very good. These examples highlighted language that had nothing to do with telling the truth. We have, in the United States, think-tanks where they think up words to put to the public so that they are completely confused. These think-tanks are hired by corporations.

For instance, the Clean Air Bill exists so you can sell your pollutants on, and so that you can continue to pollute. That's where these things come from. Every example you gave in the torture section had to do with making torture not torture, so that when it does come to light the public will not think about it. It's not a slip or something. Really smart people are hired to sit around as we're sitting around now and think this up. This is a monstrous crime and it should be stopped. Not just in my country, but in a lot of countries; everyone wants to be on the computer, in progress. This leads to a shortening up of language. There are no adjectives anymore, everything is much shorter. The preciseness of the language dwindles; the joy of the language dwindles. Everything dwindles so that these people can manipulate you more effectively.

One of the things I would add is that it's not just translation we have to watch, but the fact that this weird love of speed is making us give up our language, leaving us unable to combat them. Because we have only three words and they choose to change one word: dirty becomes clean.

David Constantine:

I think that we exist in an embattled and beleaguered condition. Unless we fight back, we're stuffed. I honestly think that. I was a teacher for 31 years and I made it my business to try to get people to write clearly. But I was in a university system that piece by piece was selling itself off to the wholly false model of business management. Universities are being overwhelmed with management-speak. So there are teachers trying to get their students to articulate critical opinions – but under a bureaucracy that wittingly or unwittingly is doing much to make that impossible. As Orwell said in 1946, poor language makes for poor thinking. A person thinking and writing poorly – unclearly, sloppily – is liable to be oppressed. We cannot answer back with bombs; as writers we answer back with effective language.

Our language has to be good. Translation, for me, is a way of enlivening my language, so that I fight better. I write lyric poems; I don't write political poems. I regard the lyric poem as an act of opposition to all the language around me that would, if let, be the death of lyric poetry.

Choman Hardi:

I'd just like to come back to the point of translation. A couple of years ago, I started translating and thinking about it seriously. Because I thought I really don't know how to do this – I'm an amateur – I took the translated poem into a workshop. In this Kurdish poem, the poet is going into exile. Towards the end there is a long stanza about his loved one looking for him in the iris of a bead, under the tongue of a dumb bird, and – in one of the lines – 'in the armpit of a wet bat'. All the translators had a problem with this; they said, well, it's wet and bat and armpit – it's really smelly. Bats are all about armpits; they hang upside down concealed in their armpits. They suggested I change it to 'under the wing of a bat,' which is very different. There is a tendency to iron things out because otherwise it sounds a bit disgusting in English, but then that phrase does sound unsettling like that in Kurdish too! You should take it playfully.

David Constantine:

An essay I read recently shows that translations are likely to be less various than their originals. Putting 'wing' instead of 'armpit' is an example of the pull towards the unexceptionable.

Jon Cook:

I think it's worth reflecting for a moment on the way in which we describe language and the act of translation as a translation of codes. What I think you're pointing to, is that strong literary language creates a space, a tension for the drawing of all sorts of inferences, all sorts of possible meanings. That seems to me to be part of the freedom that David Constantine talked about. He was distinguishing between the poet and the citizen. That moment when we are free to make inferences rather than being required to make a single sense of it. Choman's example seemed to be a very precise example of the way in which translation is taking the source language back into a highly coded version of the target language.

David Solway:

I grew up nourished in the tradition of the word. All my relatives, my grandfathers were rabbis. They studied the Torah. They believed in the word. They believed the word was magical. They put pins into the Torah where the word was that the angel resided. I grew up in that tradition.

I discovered that when I spoke to my assailants they didn't listen. When I tried to write or say something beautiful, or find a metaphor in which I could speak a certain kind of truth to them – that violence should be something to be avoided, that it is a form of oppression, a form of dumbness – it didn't work. They continued to attack me until I realized I had to fight back.

That doesn't mean I stopped writing lyrical poetry. I still write it as an act of hope against hope, and I will continue to do it. But there are times when the word, in itself, becomes useless. Or actually works against you. You said, 'you can't answer violence with violence.' I disagree. There are times when you must answer violence with violence. That does not mean that I endorse violence. Sometimes it is necessary in self-defence. I'm not an aggressive person.

Let us continue to write, let us continue to translate, let us continue to reinvigorate the language so that we can communicate more clearly with ourselves and with our fellow man but let us not forget that writing a lyrical poem is an act that, often, will have no consequence whatsoever.

There are times when the word itself becomes our enemy because we stop too long to speak it. Albert Camus wrote in an essay entitled *Algeria 1958*, 'My task is to speak clearly and to write clearly but if someone throws a bomb and my family is destroyed then I will respond in a different manner.' This is my only point.

Leila Ahmed:

When you were introducing the talk, Jon, you mentioned what languages have been dominant: English, French and Latin. I exchanged a quick glance with Aamer Hussein, because there is also Arabic. Particularly in regards to translation, it is an important underlay of the civilization that we all inhabit right now.

Regarding David Solway's comment, the one thing I would draw your attention to is that one could say you did exactly what you accuse David Constantine of. You talked about Islamic people then you brought in this example of a guy who seeks to purify the world, whom I probably hate as much as you do.

Jon Cook:

I think what this particular exchange reveals is the way in which we find ourselves using, whether we intend to or not, exactly these kind of sedimented labels and terms of classification. This goes back to something I think Luisa Valenzuela was talking about: we don't inhabit the language, language inhabits us. It seems to me that literary writing arises by being inhabited by many languages. In fact, that often makes the process of composition not something that we might think of as a creative act arising out of nothing but as something more akin to translation. That is to say you have to edit and pare back down in order to find what you need to say.

Hasso Krull:

I thought I would touch upon the dominance of English in translation from a different perspective. When I listened to what David Constantine said, I generally felt a great empathy with it. There are some things, of course, about this dominance of English that might be very hard to notice if one is living every day in an English language environment.

I thought about an interesting example: a friend, a fine woman, who is editing a bilingual, half-Estonian art review. She said that she often writes her essays in English first because it is so much easier to express her thoughts about modern art in English. The discourse is established in English; she feels very clumsy when she has to use Estonian as a first language. She or someone else translates her essays from English into Estonian.

When I saw her text, I at first thought it was a sensible text about art phenomena, artists and the world. All the key words that one has to use in English were included. It did sound a little bit vague, however. When I read the Estonian version I realized that it was only small talk – nothing was said. It was really very clumsy in Estonian, not because of any qualities of the Estonian language but because the thoughts themselves were very vague. I thought that if somebody from Scandinavia, for example, read the same text they would think: I don't really understand much about it but it is said in quite an authoritative way and there must be some meaning behind it. If someone whose first language is English read it, they would see that it was written by someone whose first language is not English. They would think they needed to read it in Estonian in order to understand it.

A vicious circle is created. I have a feeling that one can really be worried about the consequences of this dominance of English for the English language itself.

Alison Croggon:

I had a couple of thoughts about the assumption that translation is necessarily unqualified good. Personally, I only speak English, to my shame, and I'm incredibly grateful for translations for introducing me to many literatures that would otherwise not be accessible. At the same time there's an aspect I can't help but be conscious of: translation might be also a way of importing other cultures into English and owning them somehow.

I say this partly because I come from Australia. The Europeans settled two hundred years ago when there were three hundred indigenous languages in Australia; there are a dozen still spoken. Most of them have vanished with the people who spoke them. At the same time, there are some very famous translations of Aboriginal songs that indigenous people feel are a violation of their knowledge. There are all sorts of issues to do with translating across cultures. I wonder what issues there might be in particular for those who are being translated?

Jon Cook:

That poses a very interesting historical question which is, in a sense, also provoked by what David Constantine was saying in his reflections on the history of German literature. We can't think about translation in the abstract; there is undoubtedly an important historical argument that runs roughly like this: the emergence of national literatures is actually unthinkable without translation.

When you are thinking about what happens to the translation of a tribal text, for example, it seems to me that you're operating in a very different ethical and literary domain. Are we here talking about something that enriches the culture of Australia? Is it part of that business of building a national literature?

Alison Croggon:

It has been seen as such, yes. There's been a fair bit of controversy over, for example, whether Aboriginal songs ought to be included in anthologies.

Choman Hardi:

Are we talking about what it feels like to be translated into English? Well, I think, speaking from a Kurdish point of view, it's very important because if you're not translated you're not represented, and it's not just representation in terms of literature but the whole world-view. We've been talking about the ability of literature to create sympathy and understanding. History and journalism cannot do this as much. If you're not translated you don't have a voice, you don't exist. For most languages, especially endangered languages, it's very important to be translated because that means you are represented.

Eva Hoffman:

When I first started writing in English, I felt a strong sense of transgression about it. I did not feel a sense of entitlement. I thought I was transgressing on a territory that was not my own. I was going from a minority position into the dominant culture and I know that the issue of going in the other direction is very fraught and very sensitive.

I want to bring up the question: do we only have the right to write about experiences which have some immediate relationship to our identities?

I came up against this question in relation to the Holocaust. Does anybody who has not been in that event have a right to write about it? I think that anybody who has the imagination, the intelligence and the sensitivity to think about that experience should have the right to write about it. Some writings by Holocaust survivors can be very valuable as testimonies but are not very interesting pieces of writing. There are writings by writers who come from completely different vantage points which can be very interesting.

Ogaga Ifowodo:

The language question has been debated so often in African writing – *the dead end of African literature, etc.* – I'm weary of trying to talk about it. I have absolutely no apologies for using the English language. To borrow from a character in Toni Morrison's *Beloved* named Stamp Paid, I think all the colonized people of the world have more than paid for their use of the English language. It's not only the property of the English people, it is the property of all those who have paid for it.

I do acknowledge the unequal relations between English and many other languages. What are we to do? I have a choice to write in Isoko and speak to only about 1,000,000 people out of the 130,000,000 people in Nigeria. Nigeria is a linguistically imagined nation. If we didn't have that language then, probably, there'd be no Nigeria. Without English I wouldn't be able to speak to Helon Habila, even though he comes from the same country as me.

Not too long ago, English was just a vernacular language. It was the language of the barbarians. There is something that has accounted for this power that English has today; it is a power that the likes of us have given to the English language. If you think of America today – with Hollywood, Motown and CNN, and all the paraphernalia – the tools of cultural domination are extended even further. I'm glad that English can't dominate me because I can speak and write back.

I've recently been pursuing the thought that if the mother continent is Africa, and we only have, more or less, 26 phonemes, represented by 26 letters of the alphabet, ultimately all the languages of the world are my language. They spring from the first cry, the first sound or song. So I acknowledge the history of English, but I'm going to use it unapologetically and make my mark on it. Maybe in 100 years' time, English will be just another language and I hope that the people who use it then will also be happy. That said, I do not hope that all the other languages disappear, although they may still disappear naturally.

I still speak my language. After this conference I'll be going home and speaking to my 80-year-old mother in that language, but I have no apologies. The way I understand it, this cultural nationalization is only 20 or 30 years old. Although these languages have been used for many years, I hope that nobody here feels like a traitor for using English.

Mourid Barghouti:

I believe that we use language as a tool. We also agree that we are experiencing a pollution of the language, a verbicide, a misusing of the simplest words, not only in representing the strong, but in misrepresenting the weak. The idea of trying to put examples from both sides was mentioned this morning: David Constantine was giving linguistic examples, and then David Solway said that these examples were one-sided. Politicians and the Security Council can insist on such objectivity. I would love writers to be objective, but the notion of representing both sides is a euphemism for defending a status quo, and a rotten one. Because it's the strong-weak relationship. We should side with the weak, the oppressed. We are not judges, we are not judging anyone, but at least we give our sympathy to those who need it.

If my aunt says something nasty about politics, it is different from the same thing said by Dick Cheney. The words of politicians can be implemented on the ground: when they say war, then it is war. The notion of a vicious circle deflects from a very important idea: nothing starts in a circle. Something happened before something else. Something caused something. I don't blame only the politicians for the manipulation of the language; there is the unspoken language behind the spoken one. Here's a very simple example, from a review of my book: 'Barghouti was born in Ramallah, from which, as fate would have it, he was exiled.' As fate would have it? I mean, we are not discussing the fate of a UFO; I'm a person with a known date of birth, place of birth and I'm here or there because of certain historical, geographical and military events. My book does not say that fate exiled me. This word was borrowed from the hidden, unspoken language.

Language is what we do with it. Speak loudly, slowly, slangily, classically, but how? In which direction? Politicians can lie, they can call civilian death collateral damage, but this is a literary critic, one of us. It shows that the unspoken, hidden language is really dangerous.

I can't blame anyone for what is openly said. I live in Egypt, where President Mubarak runs a dictatorship, selling himself to the world as democratic. He's saying that we have freedom of press because there are many different opinions around: one pitched against the other. But this is not the freedom of the press. The freedom of the press is the freedom of the news, not opinions. Tell me what happened. They twist what happened. If they kill someone they tell you he hit his head against the wall. What shall I do with the one hundred articles of free opinion on this? I don't want them. I want to know what happened.

Be it spoken, borrowed, classical or slang, long, short or lyrical, language is a position after all. Go left, go right, go up, go down. Language exposes your stance. Those who want to hide their stance behind clichés, the big abstract nouns, will know that there are some readers, writers and decent human beings all over the five continents who will point to this as pollution of language, and as verbicide.

Choman Hardi:

I'd like to say something about writing in a language that's not your own and the responsibilities that come with that.

A couple of years ago I was on a live television programme called *Good Morning, Kurdistan* on a Kurdish satellite channel. A man phoned in. Knowing that I had been writing in English for the last four or five years, he asked me why I was on this programme. I was baffled. I had never thought that writing in English could mean that I was not really a Kurdish writer. I felt that I was recreating Kurdish in English. But then the issue of the importance of keeping our mother tongues alive cropped up. One feels guilty of that; I feel guilty if my language is threatened. It was Kant who said that if you're about to do anything, just think what would happen if everyone else did the same. Fortunately, I tell myself that not everybody else will do the same.

You're making choices: you're writing in English so you're reaching out but on the other hand you're not writing in your mother tongue. Maybe there's a sense of abandonment; there's certainly a sense of guilt, for me. There's always a hope that I will one day write in my mother tongue again.

Ogaga Ifowodo:

I certainly hope my language won't die, at least not in my lifetime. But, I sometimes wonder, before the rise of the nation, before this national consciousness and thinking within imposed borders, before our epoch, did languages die naturally? If languages are going to die, then perhaps the question to ask is why? I guess we need to worry more about the things that sustain those languages. I know of course that writing in those languages is one of the things that will sustain them. But it is not only writing that sustains a language, otherwise perhaps Latin or Greek would be more powerful than English. There are so many things that determine whether a language is going to survive, is going to be enriched, to live into the next millennium. We do our bit, in my view, but some languages are still going to die. Even English, after this triumph, could perhaps die, of course not in our lifetime or perhaps many lifetimes hence. I imagine that Caesar did not foresee Latin dying.

Austin Clarke:

The fact that we are having a *symposium* suggests to me that Latin is not dead. I speak English in Barbados but there are nuances to the English spoken in England that a Barbadian cannot understand. I'd like to return to a point of view raised earlier on: that writers like me use race as the thrust of their stories. I don't believe that a writer can do that and be successful. It may be shocking for me to admit this, but I'll give you two authorities more intelligent than myself. One is the American Ralph Ellison in his book of essays *Shadow and Act* in which he says that race cannot be the basis of any creed of art. The other one is V.S. Naipaul who singled out Richard Wright, James Baldwin and Ralph Ellison, saying that when you encounter these three, all the others are using race as the foundation for their writing.

Christopher Bigsby:

Can I just tell you a secret about the English use of English? It is sometimes mistakenly believed by people who are outside this country that we use the English language to communicate; we actually use it to avoid communication. During the war when we were threatened by invasion, we had no troops, we had nothing to fight with, the master plan was to turn all the signposts round the wrong way. The Germans would invade, follow the signposts and end up back in France. But in some ways I think that the British have never turned the signposts back the right way. We don't use language to communicate; we use it as a series of concealments, of which irony is a principal tool.

Irony is almost impossible to break through, to understand, because you're getting two messages simultaneously. I don't know how translators actually handle the doubleness of a language. Even the doubleness of a title. What's the title of *A Farewell to Arms* in French? You have to change the title completely because you can't maintain a sustainable ambiguity in the language.

We talked about entitlement. You've heard us talk about Max Sebald a lot because he was a great writer and a friend. He was in this country for forty years, yet wrote in German. I asked him why, and he said because, 'if you write a letter, you don't think about it, if I write a letter I think about it.' So he would write in German, and he would then police the English translation. At that moment I think I began to lose him because – if he was able to police the translation and have the subtlety to interrogate it – then why could he not write it in English in the first place?

The other question I have is: are books improved by translation? Is Edgar Allan Poe a better writer in French because Baudelaire translated him?

Vesna Goldsworthy:

Can I just say something from the sunny side of translation street? We heard that only 3% of literature in this country is translated. This seems a devastatingly low percentage, but actually if you live in this country it is a fantastic number of books. I speak as someone who has lived somewhere where something like 50% of published fiction is translated, but it remains a much smaller range. I really see things very optimistically. Three percentage points sounds quite devastating, but the practice of living with translation here is that masses of writers get translated. You can find an awful lot of translated books in the book shops. The issue is perhaps how to draw attention to them.

Jon Cook:

I think that one of the issues that has come to the fore is actually to do with how strong the emotions are that are carried by language. They are not necessarily emotions that I feel, or somebody else feels. They are emotions within the language itself. It seems to me that there's a very interesting question that's been circulating here about the extent to which there needs to be a certain kind of breaking from, or wrenching free from some linguistic state in order to be able to write in a literary way at all. One of the things I'd like to leave as a question, which is very pertinent to the idea of translation, is: do we mislead ourselves very seriously in thinking about our relationship to language in terms of metaphors drawn from property and ownership?

Oi khao pak chang pai laew: The cane has already entered the elephant's mouth.
This Thai phrase is typically used to describe woeful, irreversible
situations. It implies that things have already been set into motion,
consequences are impending, all one can do is watch the elephant chew.
The closest English equivalent that I can think of is, 'That ship has
already sailed,' which captures well the Thai phrase's sense of irrevocable
loss, though it fails to duplicate its invocation of the bittersweet.

I find the phrase wonderful, in a way. Like most clichés, proverbs,
and common turns-of-phrases, this one nearly bursts with unspoken
social and cultural assumptions. To state the obvious: in order for the
phrase to enter the language, its early users must have possessed at least
a passing familiarity with 1) elephants; 2) their dietary habits and
preferences; and 3) the sublime power of their masticating prowess.
Unlike that other elephantine cliché in English – which finds the
creature in the middle of rooms, and relies on mere knowledge of
the animal's size – this phrase requires far greater intimacy with the
world's largest land mammal. It posits as common the experience of
feeding an elephant; it assumes, too, that anybody who has offered an
elephant some cane, or watched the beast feed in a cane-break, knows
something about insatiability and irretrievability.

The phrase's emergence must have had something to do with an
abundance of elephants in the country's old forests, not to mention the
elephant's prominent place in a communal imaginary, where the power
of the beast was often yoked to the power of the ruling class. (Elephant
round-ups and the use of elephants for warfare and hard labour are
enduring, well-documented royal spectacles.) Indeed, the elephant's
fetishized, over-determined symbolic status seems unrivalled by any
other animal in the geographic area commonly known today as
Thailand. And while the social and cultural context that gave birth to
the phrase has largely disappeared, it is still entirely possible – if one so
desires – to feed an elephant in Thailand, to feel the strong force of its
trunk constricting around one's offering, to watch its moist, pink mouth

1. A white elephant adorned the first state-sanctioned Siamese flags in the 19th century, and, even to this day, hardly
a month goes by without some mention in the Thai media of 'unemployed' elephants wandering the capital city, after
the prohibition of elephant labour at logging camps; the construction of an elephant reserve; or the general disappearance
of the species due to poaching and deforestation. It is perhaps indicative of the elephant's over-determined status that
one begins to sense – while reading these articles – that they are not talking about elephants at all.

working swiftly at a bunch of plantains or a large stalk of cane.

I am no etymologist, lexicographer, or philologist. I am a fiction writer. And I am belabouring my point here, especially since my point has been articulated before: that language bears an enormous amount of social, cultural, and historical weight; that common, over-used phrases tend to bear more weight than most; and that their weight can hardly be registered on the scales of another language without doing violence to the phrase's ease in its original context. These phrases tend to mask consensus – however innocent, however insidious – and consensus, as a rule, requires seemingly little explanation. Indeed, in its native environs, the phrase arrives weightless, as seemingly natural as the elephants that used to roam the country's forests, as common (and therefore commonly unexamined) in Thai as letting cats out of bags, finding proofs in puddings, or putting noses to grindstones in English. It is easy on the ears.

There is that age-old translator's cliché of inequivalencies and untranslatability – where poor Hölderlin goes mad every time – and I am aware that I am approaching it here. So be it. As a writer of English language short stories set in Thailand that consistently, deliberately feature Thai characters, I believe that these concerns have some small practical consequences, and perhaps even a few political ones, most of which were discussed by other writers in much more eloquent terms during the conference in Norwich.

Since Edward Said, much has been made of the way orientalist discourses remain central to the consolidation of European power and identity. European (and American) discourses about Thailand from the 17th century onwards are certainly no exception to this hypothesis. Nearly everywhere one turns in the literature, one finds Thailand represented as radically other from the West, hyper-exoticized, and even, in some instances, grotesquely dehumanized. Though I find the prospect of pleading for Thai people's humanity inane and beside the point, I find just as troubling the vast, dehumanizing stylistic arsenal (not to speak of arsenals of other kinds) that have been trained for so long upon the region since it came into contact with Europe and America.

Much of this dehumanization, of course, happens at the level of language, of speech, and though I may find pleasure and interest in a phrase such as 'The cane has already entered the elephant's mouth' in its original, native context, I refuse to include such phrases in my English language fiction without qualification. For what may seem natural and easy in one language begins to seem awkward and false in another – begins, in fact, to seem like pure affectation. (What's more, in this instance, including the phrase would corroborate certain notions of Thai people as relentlessly 'wise' and 'aphoristic,' founts of fortune-cookie Zen wisdom – as, indeed, less than human.) It is not simply a matter of representational political correctness; it is also a matter of attempting to convince readers of my characters' believability, of their existence, which I believe to be one of fiction's primary tasks. *Nobody speaks this way,* I have often thought, during those moments when I have been seduced by the possibility of including such a phrase in my fiction, although, of course, it is in fact exactly how some people speak. It would be more precise instead to say: *Nobody listens this way.*

These are some of the problems I think about in my writing world. I have found few lasting or even adequate solutions. Each new short story seems a kind of failed experiment, though I would hope that some fail more exquisitely than others. I see no end to it. I hope there won't be one. I put it there myself, and so I'd like to keep it there, in the elephant's mouth, for as long as I am able to watch it chew.

There is another, more common elephantine proverb in Thai: *Chang tai thang tua ao baibua pit mai mit.* An elephant's corpse can't be covered with a lotus leaf. It's futile to hide a glaring, public problem once it becomes apparent. I can't think of a better argument against my fiction.

There was a time in the 60s when, if you were black, to be too English or to be too American was a cardinal sin. Derek Walcott has been criticized for being too English. There is one beautiful poem in his second collection, *In a Green Night*, called *A Far Cry from Africa*, in which he is the first black man to praise his cultural or political antecedents: the African and the English. But it is not one against the other, it is the weighing of the benefits to be derived from these two.

> How choose
> between this Africa and the English tongue I love?...
> How can I turn from Africa and live?

On the other hand, Kamau Braithwaite does not have that ambivalency at all. In the third part of his trilogy of poems, he has this political message:

> it is not
> it is not enough
> it is not enough to be free

The language that we use is like a bullet fired in the night at an object identified as oppression.

In the 60s, Malcolm X said, 'My name is Malcolm X.' Cassius Clay became Mohammed Ali and lots of blacks used their Christian names and erased the surname of their slave master, substituting it with an X, which is very ironic. An X is a symbol of luck, of being able to read and write, but the X is also the symbol for clutching independence and voting. When you vote, you vote with an X.

This is how Mary Mathilda explains herself at the beginning of my novel *The Polished Hoe*, 'My name is Mary. People in this village call me Mary Mathilda or Tilda for short.'

She situates herself as a person with connections. She is connected to a village, connected to something, whereas Nocturna is connected to a past of subjugation. Mary's not an orphan as Nocturna is.

'To my mother, I am Mary girl. My names I am Christened with are Mary, Gertrude, Mathilda. But I don't use Gertrude because my maid has the same name.'

This is peculiar, because you have a woman living in a one-person shack, employing a maid as a matter of status. The Caribbean voices send back to us our own words in a language that becomes the medium of a translation of our psychic and cultural reality. I feel to that some extent my work is bilingual.

I was in my favourite retreat in Norwich a couple of nights ago and I heard a calypso. It brought gladness to my heart in the same way as yesterday, rambling to find this place, I heard rap music coming from a huge distance, and I said to myself: I wonder if the other people listening to this understand what is going on? To hear a calypso in England and to hear rap music in England to me is the same thing as listening back home to Bob Marley or reading the fiction of Earl Lovelace, particularly his brilliant book *Salt*.

I said that we could substitute, so far as my position is concerned, domination for dominance. I said at the beginning that I was talking about language from a different point of view. *The Polished Hoe* which is coming out next month illustrates my points about language. The translation I'm thinking of is not a translation of, say, changing English into Dutch; that is too ordinary. What I'm thinking of is a spiritual translation.

Mart Valjataga
An Estonian Look at the Language Question

When writers from around the world get together for conversation, they need, as anyone does, a shared medium and a common topic. The medium of conversation is language, of course, and in our case (thanks to global trends and the location of the meeting) it is the English language. But language in general – and the English language in particular – has also provided one of the main topics.

The title of our session is *The Language Question.* In one sense the question is quite trivial: language is for literature as oxygen is for living. It becomes more complex if you think that there are many languages: 6,000 or 7,000, depending how you count. The majority of languages are minority languages. The 20 biggest languages are spoken by 80% of the world population. The average is about 1,000,000 speakers per language, but the distribution is very unequal. The Estonian language is just around the average. But many thousands of languages are spoken by less than 50,000 people. The major trend is that English is becoming the medium for communication between all the other languages.

A year ago, there was a book fair in Tallinn. The British Council had a stand there representing only authors born outside the British Isles. I visited the fair with an English journalist who later told me that the stand had a hidden message: everybody, even an Estonian, can become a British writer.

It brings to my mind a well-known parable, sometimes said to be Jewish, sometimes Oriental and sometimes Caribbean. In it, a master sends his pupil to the market with instructions to get the best thing he can find there, whereupon the pupil returns with tongue. Later, he sends the pupil to the market to get the worst thing he could find there. Again, the pupil returns with tongue. Asked how he could choose tongue as both the best and worst thing, he replies, 'There is nothing better than a tongue that speaks good, and nothing worse than a tongue that speaks evil.'

Our symposium seems to reach a similar conclusion: there is nothing better than language used in a responsible and imaginative way, as in the best literature, and there is nothing worse than language used – even in literature – for deception, domination or prattle. And more specifically: the English language is a good thing because it provides a global idiom for international communication and the expression of differences, while being a language of rich poetic tradition and vibrant contemporary fiction.

At the same time, though, there is nothing worse than a single, all-powerful language. The dominance of one language can reduce the diversity of worldviews, seduce writers into abandoning their native audience, and tempt them into developing a streamlined, international style that anticipates translation into English. In this sense, whether you like it or not, contemporary world literature is a system of inequalities. But I suppose that literary inequality and dominance is easier to bear than material or political inequality. Anyway, it is easier to share cultural than material wealth.

Probably every writer has his or her own relationship to the English language. For some, it is the mother tongue and an embodiment of a long literary tradition. For others it is a learned second language, the mastering of which has involved a conscious effort for survival in a new environment. For others again, English stirs up memories of colonial domination. It has emerged during our discussions that language, far from being a neutral medium of communication, is sedimented with collective hopes and sufferings. These vary from culture to culture, but there is a lot of overlap, too. And language can also be something of a minefield, when a euphemism turns out to be offending and the best intentions are interpreted as patronizing.

But, for me, English is not associated with any dark or painful experience, and its genius is embodied in its poetry, especially in the light or nonsense verse. So there is nothing traumatic about it (although self-expression in English is still quite an ordeal).

Writing Worlds 1
The Norwich Exchanges

Writing Futures

My theme is globalization and what it does or could do to literature. I will point to some of the opportunities and dangers it presents to writing. I find it very difficult to write as if things have not changed, the world is not global or there is no global medium of communication. I don't really know how to address globalization, but I find it difficult to ignore it and to write as if nothing had existed.

The first thing I find very challenging is the omnipresence of English. I know that, as a Frenchman, I am supposed to write about it. It's actually not so much the omnipresence of English that presents the challenge, but the emergence of a new language. When we talk about the omnipresence of English here, we are not referring to what is happening on a global scale, which is that a very particular kind of English is becoming everybody's second language. It's the English of the airport, of internet chat rooms, of video game instructions, of corporate reports, memos, emails. This pragmatic, but not grammatically perfect, English is becoming everybody's second language.

I believe it presents a similar challenge as slang presented at the beginning of the 20th century, and the vernacular later. It's a language everybody speaks. As a writer, I find it difficult to ignore. I am not saying we should write books in that language. I'm saying that we should see this as an opportunity to address the way we speak through literature. The current state of publishing makes it possible for a Frenchman like me, for example, to write parts of my book in that rudimentary English in France. I tested that idea with my French publisher. I said to him, would it be okay if I write a book half in English. He responded: What do you mean, like imitating a good English writer? I said, I will be writing like a business traveller who talks in English. My whole argument was that it would be the type of language in which someone who has been on a long plane journey has reinvented his life in, for the benefit of the person sitting next to him. It's the language in which that kind of story is told.

The second thing I find difficult to ignore is the global network, the internet, or what I call global chatter. Whenever I begin a project, I always have at the back of my mind this image of global chatter, and the fear of just adding a few more voices to it. Again, it's something I know I'm trying to engage with. I'm currently engaged on another project with other French writers, and with an engineer who listens to radio frequencies. We listen briefly to cell phone conversations. The engineer records the beginning of the conversations. We get the transcripts and use them as the beginning of our stories. The other thing that global network makes possible is the separation of texts from books. Text pours out from the page onto screens and mobile phones. Stories become a global net knitted by a thousand hands.

In that respect, your book can sometimes become a deceptive object – too finished. I don't know what to replace it with. But it's certainly something that I have been thinking about for some time. I don't have any solution, but again it's something I find difficult to ignore. The third thing I've been addressing more directly in my book, is the fact that globalization means the world is a global market. Publishing is part of the bigger industry, which is entertainment. Writing a book today means that you are part of that industry.

My first book was an attempt to address that topic. It's a novel, but it really is a user manual for a software which writes books automatically without any human intervention.

* * *

'Everything has been said.' It's time that you, entrepreneurs, use this mantra of artistic circles to your advantage. If everything has been written, filmed, and acted, if the flow of stories has effectively come to an end, it means **that narrative has finally become raw material, a commodity. Therefore, its treatment can be mechanized.** This manual will demonstrate how this can be done.

Initially in possession of one or two media, you now own several: newspapers, publishing houses, film studios, television channels, sports teams.

Consequently, **you are subjected to increasing numbers of constraints in an increasingly competitive environment.** You should be launching content which can be exploited in several, if not in every one, of your subsidiary companies.

To be profitable, a book, article or comic strip must have the potential to be rapidly converted into a screenplay, a video game or a television programme, which in turn would also be interchangeable: the ideal situation would be if all three could run in tandem. Each product is then submitted to a treatment made up of episodes, which can be rotated pretty quickly: sequel, series, foldback, revenge. Merchandizing of course would form part of the process and would include models, clothing, gadgets, etc.

You already know all this; this is bread and butter to you. You also know, faced with an increasingly vast and sophisticated market, that current **production units operate on an outdated model. The human factor is overvalued**, economies of scale are non-existent, and more often than not costs cannot be compressed.

This is for one reason only: the production line lacks continuity. Content is still manufactured in two distinctive stages: first, that which is generally referred to as the 'creation', the realm of the 'artist', and, second, the process of manipulating the content (manufacturing, marketing and distribution), which is your group's forte. The tool presented in this manual has been designed to put an end to this anachronism and, to introduce a completely integrated industrial process, one in which the conceptualization of the product is but one stage in the mechanized manufacturing process. It is ridiculous to allocate millions of dollars to the 'creation' when this part of the production process can be replaced beneficially by a judicious and systematic recycling of 2,000 years of narratives, maturing in libraries, archives, databases.

It is time to exploit rather than succumb to this accumulation of material, which makes the creators, whom you pay so dearly, giddy.

(Philippe Vasset, ScriptGenerator©®™)

It sounds ironic, but the irony is mostly on me. When I sent the manuscript out, the first publisher who said yes was the biggest publishing house in France. My publisher did exactly what I described in the book. The book is supposed to be a user manual, so I will go for it. The whole editorial process in France sounded like the rehearsal of what was in the book. It was really weird in several stages. The second joke was again on me. When the book was published in the UK, the BBC invited me for a debate, but with a scientist, not a writer. It turned out that this scientist was a guy from the MIT who had invented the software, not exactly as such (for it was not meant to save millions for publishing houses), but definitely a software that could write texts. I was somewhat stunned. The exchange was very weird, because the journalist expected me to address this problem: can computers generate texts etc? I was trying to argue that my book was a metaphor for something else, and I really didn't have an informed thing to say about how the computer could generate texts. It's possible, obviously. In a globalized world, even when you try to be ironic and funny, the joke is finally on you.

The Global Nomads: Conformity and Idiosyncrasy

In conversation: Mourid Barghouti, Gillian Beer, Ron Butlin, Amit Chaudhuri, Jon Cook, Alison Croggon, Moris Farhi, Vesna Goldsworthy, Choman Hardi, Eva Hoffman, Aamer Hussein, Ogaga Ifowodo, Kapka Kassabova, Ib Michael, George Szirtes, Mart Valjataga, Luisa Valenzuela, Philippe Vasset and Mary Woronov.

Jon Cook:

The prospect of world literature is an idea which has certainly been in circulation in European culture, and no doubt in other cultures since the time of Goethe. Our discussions earlier began to raise questions of whether we are living at that moment when something like world literature might be coming into existence.

I have been struck by Ignacio's commentary on the direction of Latin American writing, and his reaction against the idea that if you are a writer living in a Latin American country, you have to write about that country; as though it is some kind of national obligation to write about the country from which you come. There is some kind of imaginative journey whereby Latin American writers might be writing about their own country by writing about another country. Amit Chaudhuri said that postcolonial experiences are of course not only confined to countries that were once colonized. They also arise in the imperial, or the old imperial, metropolis. Postcolonial experience is happening in Britain as well as in India or, for example, Africa.

I also want to underline the sense of an international or transnational movement emerging through the number of people who have either chosen to write in English, or who find themselves within that great international circulation of writing in English. I wonder about two things: one is how much that leads to a kind of writing in which a writer from one country is free to write about another country, eluding national affiliation. The other concerns writing from within a national perspective in which the mark of nationhood is much lighter, much less aggressively loaded, much less engaged in the project of building a national literature. We may no longer be living in a time when the commitment to the building of a national literature is seen as one of the values, or cultural or political tasks, that literature might take on.

My third thought is about the media. David Constantine made a very powerful and direct statement about the relationship of literature to the media, and literature's value in caring for language. Literature has a capacity to renew and re-open the language in ways which are being endlessly closed down by media, by the discourse of politicians, and media-speak of one sort or another.

This of course puts literature in opposition to media. In the minds of certain critics, there is a war between the language of literature and media-speak, and that's where the value of literature arises, precisely because it resists the incursions of the media. We have invoked a number of quite powerful metaphors, including the notion of the contamination or poisoning of language, and have talked about literature's relationship to that abuse. It's worth bearing in mind that literature is itself a medium born out of print, and wouldn't exist without media technology.

I have been struck by the thoughts about writing in Estonia for two reasons. Firstly, because it represents writing in a language that is the language of one place and one nation only. Secondly, also because of the very striking idea of a special kind of postcolonial experience in countries where the locals are speculating on a fascination with those places where the power once resided, but has now deserted.

Amit Chaudhuri:

Philippe, would it be conceptually easier to write about the machine that produces a software that produces a story, rather than a software that produces translations? The question of translating by means of a computer was discussed yesterday. Is it possible that the whole matter of translation is a bit more difficult to conceptualize in these terms?

Philippe Vasset:

For me, the software that translates, as opposed to the software that writes books, has more potential. I like the software which is called 'Guru'. It does not generate a translation, it generates another poem.

Mary Woronov:

I believe that we are in danger of losing the imaginary and the spiritual, which is what this big monster of globalization is trying to get rid of. Globalization likes things that it can control. The best example is the art world. The world of painting is interested in inventing something new, instead of something more wonderfully imaginary. Finally, they end up with theory art, where we see words on canvas instead of that wonderful exploration. Painting has become a world of words.

I wonder why anyone would do such a thing to visual arts? The only reason I can think of is control. Art has suddenly come to represent a lot of money, and you can control something that is not imaginary. I think it's a monster that you have to look out for. I am not so open to globalization because I'm afraid of the street closing off, of people saying, this is the big street where we all have to go. I would say no. But it is there, we do have to deal with it. We had a more spiritual culture and are losing it because we believe in progress. I don't believe in any progress. Progress turns around and hits you in the back.

George Szirtes:

I think this process of globalization, the internet for example, needs not just the informative, but the idiosyncratic as well. There is quite a wide range of literature, including magazines, which deal with modernist literature. It frees one from some of the demands of commercial publication.

Ib Michael:

Using the language that everybody speaks and reads, shouldn't the English-speaking world, the literary circles and the publishers, have the obligation of bringing out original works from other parts of the world in the best possible translations? This is not the case, as we all know. As foreign writers, we get one shot, one chance. If our book doesn't immediately become a bestselling novel, we might never have another chance to be published in the English language.

The European market is closing down, everybody knows that,

everybody is protecting their own culture, and it's a tendency not only in literature. I have this idea that language dies out through lack of curiosity. One translation might contribute ideas that were never heard before; one book based on different cultural values might bring something important to English literature. Maybe we should see some publishers bringing out the translations we're talking about. You invited us, but do you really want us to be part of English literature?

Jon Cook:

You are raising a very important question. How we might approach publishers in the light of this debate is very important.

Alison Croggon:

As a poet, I am used to small margins. Talking about ideas of discourse and rupture, it's worth pointing out that the precise place where ruptures happen in literature is very individual. This is what gets lost in talking about globalization: because behind all these enormous forces and huge markets, behind all these things, there are millions of individuals.

I work in the theatre, and I've always been interested in the idea of the audience. When people talk about what the audience wants, I always wonder: How do you know? I had a conversation not long ago with someone who was informed about the fantasy genre and how it works. He said that books can be marketed. They market non-fiction books like products, like lifestyle accessories. The problem with fiction is you can't do that. Fiction books aren't cookbooks.

Mart Valjataga:

I just wanted to bring in an example of literature in the situation where there is no functioning market. In Estonia, there are less than 1,000,000 Estonian readers. There is no functioning market for Estonian literature because there is no money in it. The driving force behind writing a novel is never greed, but vanity. It's easier, for a writer, to become famous in Estonia than to become rich. Marx said that history repeats itself twice, the first time as tragedy, the second as farce. I would like to say that history repeats itself twice, first as a parody, then as the real thing. The so-called socialist bloc had an almost global literature during the Communist era, which obviously included only certain parts of the world. The only Estonian writers who could become rich through writing alone were those whose works were translated into Russian, and from Russian to many other languages, including Chinese. The Russian language was an intermediary, and Stalinist writers were translated into many languages, even English.

But of course, there are some Estonian writers who are translated into English now, and it influences their style of writing as well. If you read a sentence in an Estonian novel that says, for example, 'Tallinn is the capital of Estonia', you know it's not meant for Estonian readers. For us it is self-evident. This can produce a strange effect in Estonia as well, but I still suspect that most of it is written for an international audience.

Ron Butlin:

We touched on some of the things that conditioned how writings are sold, how they are marketed, how we see readers, how we present our writing and all the rest of it. All these ideas that we talked about have not been grounded by any representatives from the publishing side. Publishers are very strongly trying to control what's written, as we all know.

Let me tell you a short story. A friend of mine who has been published by Bloomsbury thought – like many Bloomsbury authors – when *Harry Potter* arrived, that they would all make a fortune with the trickle-down effect. We've learnt from politics that there is no trickle-down effect. What happened was that, as *Harry Potter* eroded the integrity of Bloomsbury through money, the shareholders found that they can get 15% return on their investment. They decided that writers who didn't give them 15% return will gradually be eased out. The tactful way to do it is to say we don't want a masterpiece every year, we only want a book every three years. That was pretty bad. After all, my friend has done 10 books with them so far. So much for any kind of loyalty. The next thing that happened was that she turned in her novel, they said it's great and it's good and is exactly what you are known for, but we have decided that you should move slightly into the thriller genre. Now, would you please rewrite your book? These are the points we want you not just to consider but to incorporate. We won't give you a contract until we see what you have done. That's the reality that writers who are not working at the universities are dealing with all the time.

Kapka Kassabova:

In a strange way, what Ron said is tied in with what Philippe was talking about, except that what Philippe read from his novel is an extreme version of depersonalization and commercialization. I actually have a question for Philippe, as well as everyone else. Listening to your excerpt made me think of Ray Bradbury's *Fahrenheit 451*, where he warns against the extermination of books. Even though you are talking about the extermination of human writing in your book, I wonder whether you intend this novel to be received as a kind of dystopian warning about what could happen, or as a kind of playful speculation without any particular message. Where do you see your writing on that spectrum?

Philippe Vasset:

There is so much to play with in showing what publishing can become.

Kapka Kassabova:

Do you think books like yours can contribute to this malignant process of removing writing from the person?

Philippe Vasset:

The fact that I was taken on by a big publishing house that had no problem putting my book out tells you a lot about its potential. The good thing is that once they've picked me, there is no way for them to prevent me from saying anything. When the book came out in France, in every interview, I said that the history of the book itself validates what's in it because I was taken on by a publishing house owned by a weapon trader and weapon manufacturer. I thought it would have been very arrogant for me to remove myself from everything and say that this is good, and that is bad, and that I can write outside of that; I can exclude myself from all of that.

Eva Hoffman:

I would like to look at this from the point of view of the individual's imagination and the formation of that imagination. We've been discussing the dialectic between the importance of the global and the privileged place of the local. I think we still come from a period and from cultures in which the local is extremely important. I certainly know it from myself. I sometimes think that my unconscious is geographical, and is formed by the notion of a lane which goes off into a certain direction. It's a very strong formation of the imagination, from which one is ruptured and travels to many other places. I wonder if this privileged place of the first culture, the first language, the first locality, will still hold in this more nomadic culture, in which we move between many places from earlier on. It may not have such a strong formative grip on our subjectivity. So the question is: How does one give a voice to the formation of the imagination? For a writer, the first question is how to grapple with the new condition of the imagination of the world, of the psyche; how to give it a form that somehow reflects or criticizes it.

Ogaga Ifowodo:

Maybe because in Nigeria the language of imagination is English, there isn't such a problem. Nevertheless, the kind of criticism we make of our writers, Ben Okri for example, is that he defamiliarizes and decontextualizes the grotesque in his novels. The grotesque has a history, a social parameter.

I'm wondering if going back to close reading will be the answer. The rise of post-structuralism, deconstruction and the meta-language of high theory, did a great deal of harm to literary criticism. It's a battle: those who wanted to take up literary criticism had a hard time of it when post-structuralists controlled the influential literary journals and academic publishing. It is only now that I see literary studies rising again. New Criticism in fact did most of the damage by hypostasizing literary texts, denying reference and biographies, etc. I'm wondering what could be done to go back to literary criticism.

George Szirtes:

There is a counter-argument. I want to mention the potential of moving outside the publishing area through other means and generating new life and new methods and new stories. I am from Budapest. Hungarians are all trying to get out of their language; they don't want to enrich English literature, but to get out of the Hungarian language because they feel trapped in it.

I take the example of Imre Kertész, but before Kertész there is a marvellous 20th-century poet called Sándor Weöres. Nobody knows about him because not enough of his work has been translated well enough. Imre Kertész won the Nobel Prize three years ago because he has taken his work into another language. There are people who are trapped in their language and yet they have stories to tell. Coming back to the postcolonial argument, nobody will say that you are trying to sell out by telling us about this or that district in Budapest. They would say it's wonderful because it's out there.

Vesna Goldsworthy:

In response to Ogaga's point, in some ways deconstruction is very close to the forms of close reading and the idea of high canon. It's postcolonialism that has proved so beguiling a method of reading that it pervaded feminism and Marxism and other forms of interpretation to the point that everyone just kept identifying the 'other' everywhere: I myself have been part of it. There is a certain nostalgia for formalist reading in the classroom, which we now do more and more. It's a good thing, at least for a while.

Mourid Barghouti:

In this country, there is a tendency for publishers to publish out of sympathy. Any literature that is against the regime is translated. Any writer who is persecuted in his homeland is translated. They are not the ones who have lots of novels or are valued in their own places. Publication out of sympathy, either with an agenda or with good intentions, jeopardizes the quality of literature.

Amit Chaudhuri:

I don't want to present globalization as a homogenous entity, but I do think it's worth thinking about processes of homogenization which marginalize the random. I wrote about Indian poet Arun Kolatkar who died last year. He is the one Indian who wrote in English who devoted himself completely to transforming the ordinary, the shabby and the derelict into something compelling.

His book was published four or five years before *Midnight's Children*, in 1976. He stands for me at a juncture: Indian writers could have gone on that way, or they could have followed the route which Rushdie did; which concerns the architectural history of huge monuments. In one of his books, Kolatkar talks about places of worship that have fallen and are full of puppies and cats. He would give away the charge of witnessing historical monuments for the philosophical. What happened is that certain historical buildings in Indian history textbooks were iconicized after independence. Before independence, in the early history textbooks, Kolatkar says that those icons have random images in front of them, be it a dog, a horse, an animal, a man on a bicycle, etc. Afterwards, it's only the building that remains, emptied of the random. National images are turned into sacred images.

Something similar happens in Hollywood: the random gets more and more marginalized. For example, in a film, we see two men talking to each other on a cliff looking over the precipice, they drink and throw the bottle down the precipice and a few seconds later, we hear the glass break. This is the random and this is what films can do. We don't have that today. Whenever we speak out for the random, we are also aware that to speak of the romantic is to get dangerously close to the organic. Because the organic, the poetic, has been beloved of all kinds of political persuasions which we know to be destructive.

Which is why I think literary criticism is shackled. It is shackled by what happens in Western history. The question we have to ask is, when we speak out for art, are we going to make art responsible for what we did in history? That is, is there anything wrong with the romantic rupture, the quasi-transcendental quality? For example, Hitler liked certain kinds of music and collected the kind of music that was both organic and fascist. Within every good idea, you will find a political affiliation or lineage that is problematic. Are we going to make art responsible for history? Which is what we are doing. Is it therefore true that we can no longer speak for art, because we find that art has always been involved in such problematic lineages? We have to come out of that. We have to step out of our inability to speak for art because of the problematic lineages.

Aamer Hussein:

I would like to talk about the rediscovery of my mother tongue. To appropriate what Luisa Valenzuela has said more than once, I have inhabited several languages in writing and speaking, with various degrees of fluency. Three scripts run in my head, and one of them is from right to left, which can cause problems of vision sometimes. This means all my works are varied, not just my writing world. I prefer to think in terms of natural rather than national language. Sometimes I do wonder whether England has become my home as the language comes to me through education, or whether I think in English primarily because I'm in England. In terms of place, I have been aware of the importance of 'the first place'. For me, the 'first place' was rediscovered when I was about 30. I only really took possession of this place when I returned to it in my 40s, and it became the place for which, and about which, I write. This is not intentional in any way.

In discussing the choice of language, I have to accept that my native language was invented before the British developed theirs. In Pakistan today, regional language is prevented from growing, and regional writers from expressing themselves. The choice of English is therefore sometimes an election to go sideways. In the past few days, we heard an Estonian, an Argentinian, a Frenchman, a Croatian and so many others use subtle, intricate English, giving us a rich glimpse into the dimensional landscape of writings in English.

As a writer born in Pakistan and living in London, I'm a post-colonial writer, and now, frequently, an exiled writer because I live in one place and write about another. I'd like to talk about some classics translated from Persian to English which some of you might not even have heard of. These works are available in Penguin Classics. I would like to ask you to seek them out. I'll leave you with a brief quote from a poet friend of mine, urging you 'to accept the difference on its own terms'.

Jon Cook:

There is the context of a contemporary version of slang, this extra-territorial English which inhabits human speakers as well as machines, which you can encounter anywhere in the world. What Philippe is suggesting is a kind of global slang, and he is writing a text in that global slang. The writing of literary texts in more than one language is a practice that was evident before the industry of literature developed. There were texts in the Roman Empire, for example, poems in Latin or some form of Latin – the Macaronic – which were modulated into a kind of speech. It's a very interesting proposition. Because of the identity of a nation inhabiting a language, and the literature written in the language of the nation, we don't tend to think of the possibility of a literature written in more than one language.

Gillian Beer:

Charlotte Brontë, in *Villette*, quite freely wrote in French.

Jon Cook:

We think about the condition of the present and the possibility for the future. Something in the past is illuminated because of something to do with the future. This is interesting in relation to the idea of tradition, and the ways writers spoke to us about their personal or invented traditions.

George Szirtes:

You can only do this in some international languages. There is no great point for me to start interjecting in Hungarian.

Gillian Beer:

But if you are reading aloud, then there would be the point.

Jon Cook:

George has read me a wonderful Hungarian version of *Kubla Khan*. An interesting aspect is the estrangement: within the context of the language that you know, the language that you don't know.

Vesna Goldsworthy:

This creates a certain exoticism which isn't expected to be translated or footnoted.

Jon Cook:

It's interesting to see how some writers do footnote their texts with translations of a vernacular. It's an interesting literary decision, whether you want to footnote your writing or not.

Luisa Valenzuela:

Footnotes are so unpleasant in literature, except when you play around with them. Otherwise the works sound too academic. But what is interesting here is mobility, brought about perhaps by globalization and migration. There are very notorious examples here in England, yet there must be many more migrants or children of migrants who are producing in English a literature that is exciting and different. But there is not yet a school of reading for these texts, as when Spanglish made its appearance in the US. Languages are constantly enriched by foreign incorporations. Hybridization can be very interesting, yet it has to be extremely well done, and reviewers have to realize it is not minor literature but something perhaps new. I don't know how much postcolonial theory can help here. Or how much the market interferes with experimental writing.

George Szirtes:

I spoke Hungarian for my first eight years. I came to England and then I started to think and write in English. I went back to Hungary in 1984. By then I had a few books published. After 1984, I started to be seen as a Hungarian poet, but I hadn't written a word in Hungarian. I'm very wary of the way, for example, a Hungarian poet puts a few street names in Hungarian and puts some rhymes in so that now everybody knows how to pronounce those names.

I'm talking about the position of comfort, leisure, and superfluity. To some of us, it's not a question of superfluity, it is a vital question. On the one hand, you want to play, on the other hand, you are constrained to play simply by deriving your experience from these languages in a different direction. Some of us here write in a second language. These are not purely abstract things.

Moris Farhi:

There is the sense of loss – some of us have lost languages that have rich literature. People who write in different languages are almost schizophrenic. This is a type of schizophrenia that is very valuable because somehow we immerse our previous cultures with the new cultures. There has been great work in every language, what we can see is pea-sized. Because there is such great literature in every language, I feel that we should keep on translating more and more.

Luisa Valenzuela:

I am very grateful to the English language. Otherwise I wouldn't be here today. But at some point I decided I couldn't face a total immersion in it and chose to go back to my country. I needed the Argentine accent as background music to be able to move on with my writing. Shifting languages is something very special, but I felt it would constrain me because my English vocabulary is not rich enough. Though I remember hearing a Russian poet say he was very happy when he started writing poems in English because he couls freely use foul words and mention very sexual matters without feeling obscene. Those words had no emotional connotation for him so he felt free. On the other hand, a New York poet confessed that, when he started to write in Spanish at an adult age, his poetry changed, becoming very intimate and homey because he was recovering childhood memories.

And again, there is the example of Spanglish. With the grammatical use of their two tongues overlapping, the Latino writers in some way are creating a new Romance language. They are moving away from both English and Spanish, and reinventing a whole new literature.

Choman Hardi:

When I started writing in English, there were a few of us 'refugee writers'. There were quite a few established writers who were trying to get translated into English. Nobody was really interested in them. Many of these writers did not have the linguistic skills to translate their own work. But things have improved now and some of these writers have gone on to be published, to be translated properly. I think another barrier has been broken. I was an established writer in my language and it felt that I was secluded in one language while I spoke and read in another. When I started writing in English I read in small venues like libraries and bookshops where four people turned up. Now I get invited to festivals and read to bigger audiences. I still think there are other barriers which are worth bringing up.

There is the issue of mainstream literature and what it represents. David was saying the other day that there are different kinds of exciting literature being written in Britain, and he is proud of that. I think that's true but the mainstream literature scene does not recognize or represent all of them. By this I mean the reviews, selections, nominations and prizes do not reflect the different kinds of literature in Britain. They need to include writers who are not mainstream to carry forward the diversity.

Aamer Hussein:

When does this question of faithfulness to the language come in? I would like to bring back the notion of natural language. When does a language become natural to you, after how long?

Luisa Valenzuela:

I don't think it's a question of being faithful to a language, not even the mother tongue. As writers, we have to betray our tool as much as possible. I think my span of thinking in my own language is much larger, as I can handle and play with words and be more creative. I don't feel at all free in English, and if I had chosen to change languages as, for example, the Puerto Rican Rosario Ferré did, I would have been much more constrained in many ways. I wouldn't have been able to 'betray' the language in its own domain, I would have had to be careful and respectful and boring. So, I think my two most important moves were leaving Argentina in 1979 and returning in 1989; both were in defence of my writing. I moved out during the military dictatorship: I had to escape not so much for my life as because I wanted to keep on writing. After writing one long story which I was afraid of showing even to my friends – it could put the reader in some kind of danger – I feared the next step would be to stop writing altogether (this is what censorship can do to you). So I went away and decided to stay away as long as possible. Ten years later I returned home to defend my writing once more, for I was facing a wholly different strain – the change of language. I didn't feel good about it. Not because of faithfulness, but because of comfort.

Ron Butlin:

In Scotland, with our two languages, there is a sense of commercial censorship. As a writer who writes in both languages, I know English publishers won't touch it if I write in Scots. Scottish publishers will think that it is fascinating, but they won't want to take the writing and sell it in England. In Scotland, people will think it's a bit parochial. So whether or not they are going to be true to their mother tongue, which is Scots, is a real decision for a lot of writers in Scotland. I try to fit it in where it can be fitted in, or otherwise I'll not be published. This is what one Scottish poet once said, 'I think in English, but I feel in Scots', and I wonder how many people here share this experience with their own language.

Amit Chaudhuri:

The story of official language is the story of humanism and morality. You see the same story with Bengali in pre-independence India. You can see the corruption of Bengali by English, and English by Bengali. In future discussions I wouldn't want the question of cultural diversity to be always located in the context of stories in English, and the way it creates hybrids. We now know about other cultures through a group of postcolonial writers. Although we don't necessarily know what their traditions are, those traditions create the richness of those cultures. Those cultures are not rich because they are writing about the Empire, but because they are adapting their own inheritance.

Amit Chaudhuri
Why Are You Writing About This Street?

I am thinking, listening to Philippe and taking in this idea of a computer that writes novels, of a book that I read a long time ago by the Indian writer R. K. Narayan. The book is called *The Vendor of Sweets*. The protagonist is a sweet seller in Madras, his son has gone to America and comes back married with an American wife who earns a living on a story-writing machine she has invented. I think that's a response to Narayan's own travels to America, to the invention of the creative writing school. The whole idea of the story-writing machine might possibly be a metaphor for what might have seemed to him like the manufacturing of writing; but, of course, the question of what happens to writing, to language, even to the reader, and in what ways each of these is invented, becomes an altogether different one in the age of globalization.

Yesterday, we heard David Constantine's very moving talk. He spoke about the process of estrangement, of defamiliarization in poetry and in art – a process that's not only disappearing from writing, but which we are also, as readers, losing the capacity to recognize. I gave a talk recently in Cambridge entitled *The East as a Career;* a reworking of a phrase which serves as an epigraph to Edward Said's *Orientalism*. The epigraph itself, 'The East is a career,' is a quote from Disraeli. Disraeli was obviously speaking (rather sardonically) at, and of, a time – the 19th century – when the East was a career for certain English writers: Byron, Moore. It's intriguing that more than 100 years later, the East is seen to be a career for Indian writers who write in English. Leaving aside for a moment whether or not the East is a career, whether any given subject can be a career, and how that career might take shape, given globalization, given the market, the response itself to that career is interesting for its own sake.

For instance, in India, there are nativists who are against people writing in the English language, and what the Indian English writer is criticized for is seemingly selling his culture to the West. What he gets accused of, then, is 'exoticizing' his subject for a Western audience. Two questions keep coming up, 'Which audience are you writing for?' and 'Are you exoticizing your subject for a Western audience?'

One interesting thing that I notice here is that, post-Said, post-*Orientalism* (Said's works have been liberating in many ways and limiting in others), the postcolonial critic in India has developed a language with which to detect 'exoticism' or cultural misrepresentation in a literary work, but no literary language with which to deal with estrangement or 'defamiliarization' (and here we return to, but by a very different route, the point David Constantine had raised.) The 'foreignness' inherent in the exotic is confused with the 'foreignness' brought about by literary estrangement: both are, of course, literary effects, but in what they assign significance to, they're radically different from, even opposed to, one another. There is a certain kind of writing for which the lifeline is the transformation of the commonplace or the mundane into the extraordinary: to deal with what is happening in such a text, you need a critical language that is alive to defamiliarization. In India, where critical language is increasingly a postcolonial, post-Saidian language and deals with the politics and sociology of cultural misrepresentation, with the transactions surrounding the circulation of images between East and West, with 'selling' culture, the questions a writer who writes about locality, who writes, say, about a familiar street might be asked are: 'Why are you writing about this street? We already know about this street. Are you doing it because you want to sell it to a reader who doesn't know about the street?'

In post-independence India, especially in the last 20 years, I have to say that, sadly, critical discourse has abandoned the business of finding a language with which to understand the process by which writers make the ordinary not ordinary; indeed, it has conflated that process of investing the familiar with the quality of 'foreignness' with a different kind of foreignness, that is weighted with the Foucauldian idea of the pact between knowledge and power. And this has had a most impoverishing effect on literary discussions in India. This is where postcolonial discussions seem to critique global markets, but by being blind to estrangement, to the constant imaginative renovation and complicating of the 'local', they play into globalization's own disavowal of 'place'; its own blindness to the workings of defamiliarization.

I completely agree with Philippe that we can't, in our critique of globalization, pretend it doesn't exist or that it never happened. At the same time, I feel deeply ambivalent about what globalization does to our readerly and writerly practices. My values and my whole belief in the value of literature and defamiliarization come to me from a certain modernist frame of mind, which I have to say has a significant, even central, history in India. There is a 150-year-old tradition of modernity and modernism in India which Indian intellectuals, for various reasons, haven't persuasively theorized yet. It's not as if we went straight from the spiritual and mystical to the politicized postcolonial. We passed through a period of civilization which is also located in the modern. And it's important to recall that it was in the context of the modern and the humane that the anti-imperialistic movements took place, not in the context of the postcolonial and the anti-enlightenment. Given this history, the residues of which were formative of my own consciousness, I suppose I cannot help feeling ambivalent about post-modernity, globalization and certain aspects of post-structuralism, even as I feel liberated by some of these things.

In some ways, these three categories seem to have fundamental continuities with each other. Post-modernity, globalization, post-structuralism: post-modernity and post-structuralism being either moments in time or periods in philosophy or the way we look at the world, in which, suddenly, discourse or textuality seems to take over everything. Whether it is a man writing a book, a machine producing a story, or the text in a message, the implication is that there isn't that much of a hierarchy separating the man in his creative act from the text message. What is interesting here is the whole tendency towards the continuous, the discursive, the narrative, and the idea that there is no 'outside' to narrative or textuality. To me, the idea of walking down a road and discovering a lane going off somewhere inspires a childish fascination about the unknown. This is the outside I'm talking about, the rupture, which is a moment so constitutive of the world before post-modernity. In a global world, there is no unknown lane. You feel that everything has been domesticated in the global discourse, in its intricate, lateral (rather than vertical) network of economic and political transaction; even, or especially, in the domain we call 'information.' Whether by internet or by satellite or the numbers on our credit cards, we now know that there is no part of the world, not even the most remote part of Afghanistan, that isn't being watched or recorded or which, necessarily, can't be traced.

Two years ago, I was in America. I was on one of those Greyhound buses going out of New York. This was a rehearsal of a kind of journey once mythologized in numberless road movies, songs, and, in literature, of course, by Jack Kerouac: the quest for anonymity as you pursue the highway, the opening on to the 'outside'. But the romance doesn't work anymore. There is no anonymity or opening; the moment you use your credit card while buying something at a gas station, or make a call on your mobile, you are inserting your identity into a text that already exists. Here, it's interesting to see how unipolar globalization, the economic and political system in which we live now, and post-structuralism and post-modernity all come together in the idea of one continuous discourse to which there is no outside. It is here that I feel that we must look anew at our roughly 20-year-old celebration of storytelling; that, in the new context of our unipolar, free market universe, we perhaps need to be somewhat sceptical about storytelling as an unambiguously triumphant idea.

The idea of narrative, the idea of telling stories, fits in extremely well with the métier of globalization. What gets marginalized, indeed, is that moment of rupture, which poetry constitutes. Defamiliarization, the moment of rupture – these are areas of aesthetic and cultural experience that don't quite preoccupy the theory of literature today (despite significant gestures towards the 'rupture' in Derrida); that theory, it seems, must constantly grapple with or enunciate ideas of discursiveness, whether it's nation, whether it's the global, whatever it might be – even Derridean *écriture*, which, with its relentless dismantling of the transcendental signified, its endless deferral of the signified, does away with the 'outside', and becomes one of the philosophical co-ordinates that prepares the way, seamlessly, for the text of globalization. When does storytelling begin to collude with the continuity around us? And when does it stop valorizing those moments of rupture which are so important to breaking down that continuity?

Here I come to the novel – the rise and rise and rise of the novel. Among the things I find very interesting about England are the deprecating, anxious noises made every few years in literary circles about some unpopular person usually, like Naipaul, saying that the novel is dead; the chattering set go on to note with satisfaction that he still went on to write another novel the following year. I came here to England and was watching a programme on television about books; a plug, really, for the Hay-on-Wye festival. Three novelists whom I actually admire as writers, Jonathan Coe, Kazuo Ishiguro and Julian Barnes, were discussing their own novels and the novel in general. Then came the inevitable question: Do you think the novel is dead? The three concluded that the novel is actually doing well, as if it were a controversial subject that had once more been settled or put to rest, as if lots of people had thought that the novel had been in a diseased state but had been waiting for a certificate of health, which had now been given. It seems very odd to me that a genre which is really a tyrant should need a periodic certificate of health. Why should we go through with this ritual of pretence – to do with whether the novel's fortunes are failing or not, to do with whether it's sick or well – when other genres are actually getting buried in this country: poetry, the short story, the essay?

This is another corruption of language; mirroring the corruption of language by Foreign Office spokesmen that David Constantine was talking about, vis-à-vis Iraq and Palestine. Our anxiety about the novel's health seems to be akin to powerful and unwittingly ironical rituals in tyrannized communities where people – or a chorus – raise nervous prayers for the long life of the despot; it deflects our attention from the fact that the novel, the despot, is overtaking everything. This is as much a corruption of language as the claim that we are reading more and more, that more and more people are buying books. If you go to a bookshop in England today, you'll know very well that the situation's very different from what it was 10 years ago. You know that only a certain kind of book gets sold at Waterstone's.

And now, another instance of language being corrupted, or, at least, reinvented. Let's think of the reinvention of literary language (as we've discussed the reinvention of political language, how, in that reinvention, political language is made fictional, similarly, literary language becomes, in a sense, political); the language by which, until about 25 years ago, critics evaluated and analyzed literature. The whole language of speaking of masterpieces, great novels, great works of art, we know, for various ideological reasons – and many of them have to do with history, the Second World War, Fascism, etc. – that this language has been neutered; deconstructed for its absolutist and foundational biases by literary departments, which have now, inevitably, become cultural studies departments, dealing, for the most part, with the sociology of signs. Where has literary language gone? It's gone to the publishers and the agents, it's they who have appropriated the idea of the masterpiece. It's not at all unusual today to be told by a publisher that a novel they're *about to publish* is a masterpiece. The actual people who are supposed to go through, over a period of time, the strenuous, argumentative and traumatic process of literary judgment are elided, reduced, or, better still, simplified: in the meanwhile, literary theory has left open the field to the market, to globalization's reinvention and appropriation of narrative.

But there is no critique of this reinvention. There is only a dogged and dated critique of hierarchy; a particular critique of hierarchy which we don't need anymore because, in postmodernity, hierarchies have relocated and radically reframed themselves. This is the thing about hierarchies and absolutes; they are not only static – they are at once static and fluid, and their absoluteness is not incompatible with their constantly taking on new guises; becoming, even, their own opposite as they do so.

We do need to take popular culture seriously; we also need to reframe a language to understand what 'popular' culture means in the context of the present – for the word, like 'freedom', has been re-formed and almost made theological in the unipolar world. How do we develop a critique of the global, without at the same time pretending that globalization hasn't happened? We can't have a critique which says, 'All this is terrible, globalization is bad, let's go back'. We don't want to go back; at the same time, we have to make our knowledge of globalization, of discourse, of power, negotiate, in a way different from ever before, the close reading, the specificity, that gave us pleasure.

Our First Readers

In conversation: Christopher Bigsby, Ron Butlin, Austin Clarke, Jon Cook, Alison Croggon, Choman Hardi and Mary Woronov.

Christopher Bigsby:

The question of the first reader always interests me. In one sense, the first reader is the writer, but then we have the agent or the editor. In this country, for the most part, the notion of editor has virtually disappeared; the notion of editor receiving the work, that is, and working on it in detail, modifying it and changing it, etc. The editor used to be a crucial figure. Is it still true that reading that comes back from the editor remains crucial, or is it the job for the writer to resist?

Ron Butlin:

For me, the most important people who read my work are friends who are also writers. Then I get the feedback from them without an agenda. The feedback I get from agents and editors is related to marketing, whereas my friends are trying to help me do the best I can.

Christopher Bigsby:

Austin, when you finish a novel, do you hand it over or do you expect this moment to be the beginning of a process?

Austin Clarke:

My last work was accepted before it was seen. The editor was a friend of mine. When he did see it, it was 1,160 pages long. I work in a cocoon. I don't show my work to anybody. I showed my work once to my wife who was a head nurse. I woke her because it was three o'clock in the morning. After about half an hour, she came out and said, 'are you still writing the same shit?' I never showed my work to my wife again and, of course, she didn't remain my wife for long. I don't show the editor until the book is finished.

Christopher Bigsby:

There are writers who will send a chapter to an editor on a regular basis. Some quite distinguished writers rely on the feedback in the process of writing. I'm not sure if that's true for anyone here.

Mary Woronov:

I will start telling parts of my story to anyone to get a reaction and to hear myself go through it. Being an actress, this comes easily to me.

Austin Clarke:

To discuss the novel I'm working on with anybody will spoil the sacredness.

Alison Croggon:

When I write poetry, I feel that the only person I need to please is myself. I want to make a form that pleases me. To me, this is a very private thing. I show it to my partner sometimes. I am displeased if people I show don't like it. On the other hand, I worked in the theatre where I would finish a text and then give it to the people there, and be prepared for the changes.

Christopher Bigsby:

You mentioned theatre, which is worth invoking. I remember Harold Pinter came here after he had done a script for *The French Lieutenant's Woman*. I asked him if, when, the script was presented to them, he changed it at all. He said, 'well, Meryl Streep said something to me', there was this long pause, then he said, 'not anything interesting.'

Doris Lessing and John Fowles both receive lots of letters and both like receiving letters. When the novel is written and it goes out there, what happens then? In the theatre, you can see the audience's response. With the book, you have no sense of the quality of response except through the business of readings, which have emerged in the last 20 years. I don't know if that's a universal phenomenon, that the writer is expected to be a public reader?

Mary Woronov:

I've had people saying, 'you read very well, why don't you read my story?' Maybe they're right, maybe actresses should give the readings in place of the author.

Choman Hardi:

Writers need a bit of coaching sometimes, especially for private events. They just have one chance to present their work to their audience and, if they are terrible readers, maybe they need to hone their performance skills, especially the poets.

Jon Cook:

The British Museum has gathered together recordings made by poets reading their own work. The earliest recording was that of Browning. In the 19th century, writers were already making records of themselves reading their poems. I am fascinated by the way in which the recording enabled him to bring out a certain kind of musicality in his poetry, the musical notation that he worked out. We tend to think of it as something that might detract from literary value; in fact, it might be adding to the value of the work.

Christopher Bigsby:

The audio book has professionalized the idea of reading.

Jon Cook:

It's valuable because it democratizes the experience of literature.

Christopher Bigsby:

With poetry, it was always there. It wasn't with the novel, apart from the 19th-century performer-writer.

Mary Woronov:

The oral tradition, the telling of stories does live on in other countries. In our world, we are almost afraid of the oral tradition. I think it's great that books on tape are coming back.

My Writing Worlds:
Authors Talk about Their Work

Lisa Appignanesi

It occurred to me that my work seems to coalesce around two poles, which might just be a contrapuntal dance around the same one.

One is how the migrating self is written, the forgettings that are also memories, the ruptures as well as the linkages that the making of stories brings into being. Some of these stories probe back into childhood – though that early reconstructed self, often the self of another language, may be the seat of lies as well as truths. This is very much the terrain of my last two books, the family memoir, *Losing the Dead*, and *The Memory Man*. Both are concerned, differently, with how memory, which is in a sense, experienced history, plays through families.

My thrillers and more popular fictions – *Sanctuary, The Dead of Winter, A Good Woman, The Things We Do for Love* – couched in a pacier idiom, are about the surprise of Others, the way one never really knows them, their startling deceptions, their hidden-ness. Or is this, perhaps, how the migrated self feels in a world which is never quite familiar enough?

And then, of course, with my non-fiction, there is all the interest in mind, its unconscious side, psychoanalysis.

Mourid Barghouti

Life will not be simplified. Oversimplification is my enemy as a poet. In the last 50 years, life in my part of the world has been a braid of the normal and the abnormal. People pursue their everyday life amidst historical extremities of war, emigration, oppression and uncertainty. In my work, I attempt to defy the conventional language by which this unconventional world is described; I try to see the astonishing in the usual, and the usual in the extreme; the main paradox of Palestine being that bombardment is less news than a family reunion! Formally too I am fascinated by this braid of the usual and the unusual. Just as war and peace express themselves in the number of family members present at the breakfast table, I attempt to express the strangeness of my world in words that are not strange at all. I want my language to be physical, precise, visual, concrete, daily and normal, just to reveal how abnormal the condition it describes is. In doing this, I attempt to suggest a new language that defies the fake and flamboyant governmental grandeur, aimed at belittling complex reality by a flat two- dimensional metaphor. No theory terrorizes me, life is richer than all our ways of writing it and a beautiful poem can turn all literary theories upside down.

Ron Butlin *The Importance of Imagination*

One of the first times I went into a school to give a writing workshop, a girl put up her hand saying she'd written something, 'I'm not sure if it's a poem or not.' She showed it to me, and the two lines she'd written allowed me a deeper glimpse into life than many novels, 'Sometimes I know I'm bigger inside / than outside.'

Since then, I've begun every writing workshop with the same question: What do you really need to have if you're going to write a story or a poem? There is one constant and alarming trait: the older the age group (playful pensioners excepted!), the longer it takes to come up with the obvious answer. I once led an in-service with an educationalist who managed to talk for an entire hour on creativity without once mentioning imagination.

The reader I regard as my collaborator – bringing their imagination to the words and creating their own unique version of the poem or novel. The older, or perhaps the more educated we become, the less we seem to value imagination. Yet, it is at the very heart of who we are: if we lose touch with our imagination, we're lost – as individuals and as a society. End of story.

Austin Clarke *The Language and* The Polished Hoe

The narrative of this 'new writing world' must be delivered in the first person. It would be spoken by a woman, not a man. And it would have to be conveyed, in its language, its etymology and its psychic peculiarity, either primarily in 'nation language' (formerly referred to as 'dialect'), or in a watered-down version of nation language coupled with traditional English, in a deliberate 50-50 blend. In other words, I wanted to invent a new language for *The Polished Hoe*, and to creolize Oxford English.

Something similar to what Patrick Chamoiseau achieved so brilliantly in his novel, *Texaco*, bending the syntax of the French language to the nuances and linguistic culture of the French-speaking Martinique peasants.

But I wanted to go a step farther. I wanted to make my main character, Mary-Mathilda reclaim her dignity, her character, her African personality. And in doing this, I wanted her to achieve the victory of finding her voice, of creating this new language, and thus achieving her freedom.

David Constantine

I have published several volumes of poetry, the most recent being *Collected Poems* in 2004. I also write short stories, and plays for radio. My academic work was in German literature, and I have translated prose, poetry and drama by Goethe, Hölderlin, Kleist, Brecht and Enzensberger. I am co-editor of *Modern Poetry in Translation*. Translating good foreign literature into English is one way of combating the insularity and xenophobia of the nations whose native language is marching towards hegemony.

I believe in a Republic of Letters that extends across the frontiers of space and time. It is a republic in this: that it cares for the *res publica*, for our common lot. It is local and cosmopolitan. Above all it is, in Louis MacNeice's phrase, 'incorrigibly plural'. Its language, especially its poetry, seems to me an effective way of answering back. And we do need to answer back. We need a language fit and able to contradict those people, for example, who have begun to call torture 'enhanced interrogation techniques', the words making the deed more doable.

Alison Croggon

I'm glad this title is plural, because I have several writing worlds. My childhood is already fragmented: I was born in South Africa of English parents, returned to England when I was four and have lived in Australia since I was seven. This very 20th-century biography means that I am not quite native anywhere, although Australia is my home. I have sometimes wondered if this is why the worlds I inhabit imaginatively through reading and writing are so compulsively various – I can't seem to do just one thing. Or perhaps it is a variant of Borges's observation, that every writer creates his own genealogy, and that I'm still looking for mine.

Every piece of writing is a world in itself, and creates worlds around it. My personal writing worlds are various – the theatre, poetry, fantasy and other fiction, critical writings of various kinds – and then there are all the worlds one builds and discovers in one's reading. Writing leads both inward, into contemplation, and out into the wider world. I am fascinated that the tensions of writing and reading are so often such solitary activities, and yet simultaneously inherently social and communicative. For me all these worlds interlink, both contradicting and augmenting each other – writing is active and political in the world in ways that are hard to trace but nevertheless profound. I am fascinated by the relationships and dialogues that writing expresses, all these ways of making and finding meaning.

Moris Farhi

In the main, my work concentrates on the plight of persecuted peoples and threatened cultures. Given much of the world's obsession with nationalism and political 'utopias', these minorities not only face disenfranchisement, but are also in danger of dying out either through enforced assimilation or ethnic cleansing or, at its most extreme, genocide. For, as Nazism, Communism (Soviet and Chinese), the plethora of dictatorships in most parts of the globe and the Iranian theocracy have tragically demonstrated, the quest for 'utopias' always creates monolithic structures, always imposes totalitarian or fundamentalist systems where pluralism, cultural diversity and individuality cannot be tolerated.

I passionately believe in the need for political and moral maturity that will so improve the human condition that we can (as a character in my latest novel, *Young Turk*, advocates) 'rejoice in the infinite plurality of people as we rejoice in the infinite multiplicity of nature; renounce single cultures, single flags, single countries, single gods and embrace – and preserve – every culture, every race, every faith, every flag, every country, every god for its difference and uniqueness.' So healed we can be both citizens of our countries and citizens of the world, both an individual and everybody.

Xiaolu Guo

My eyes stand at the edge of my notebook and my cup of coffee, and once again I ask myself if it is necessary that an author should resist her own presence in her novel. Why not just embrace the characters? I close my eyes and let the sound of the sea seduce me, and I feel I am naked walking into the sea.

How close can the author be towards her characters? An author sometimes is an aged man waiting on the death bed, or sometimes a little girl holding a red poppy in the fields, or simply can be a bird or a piece of rock. Such a great job, probably the best job, in the entire human history. Some writers use brain to write, while others use heart. And the clever ones use both. I've been the writer without brain for many years. For that, I only used my heart to write, and my inner emotional world always flooded my social sensibility.

I write in Chinese. Three years ago I moved to England. Resident in London, I finally realized writing is such a geographic thing. So I start to use brain to draw the map of the stories. *Village of Stone*, and my new novel *A Concise Chinese English Dictionary for Lovers*, are the result of living in the West as a native Chinese. Thank God, I didn't change very much from being abroad. I am still very emotional with no logics at all. I deeply love and also respect a kind of special quality in the writing world, the quality of sharpness and intimacy.

Helon Habila

As an African writer I grew up with the notion that all serious writing must be dedicated towards some national or political agenda. This belief can be a big weight on a writer – it can work in two ways. One, it can give a writer's work a high sense of committedness and seriousness and ultimately save him from frivolity. It can also make him a sort of icon in the eyes of his readers and fellow countrymen. But two, it can narrow his field of creativity, and if the writer is not very talented his work begins to assume the feel of a political pamphlet.

I have been living outside my country for over three years now, and gradually I am beginning to question the truth of political fiction in the narrow sense – this, as I've mentioned above, is a very big issue in African and postcolonial fiction. But my growing conviction, not very original, is that the writer's duty is to illuminate the human condition, and it is his choice what set of circumstances he uses to do that. In any case, his political writing isn't immediately going to change the political reality of his time and place.

Eva Hoffman

I came to the world of writing quite late, largely because of emigration. I left Poland for Canada when I was 13, and subsequently went on to the US to study, and begin my professional life. I was a young enough immigrant so that acquiring a functional command of English came relatively easily. But it took much longer for the language to seep into the psyche; it took longer still for me to feel that I was entitled to write in this acquired tongue, or that I could develop a voice in it, or that it could possibly be heard among so many others.

The culture which matters most is the culture inside – the culture which has actually entered and shaped our inner world. My writing is necessarily infused by the subliminal tonalities of Polish and the more conscious valences of English; by the landscapes of Cracow, New York and now London, in which I grew up, and by which I continue to be formed. I sometimes think the unconscious is geographical, and its mappings diagrammed by the places and weathers we have deeply known.

Since I came to writing late, I'm in a good position to gauge the transformation it has wrought in my life. Writing is simultaneously the most private and the most public of activities. In its private guise, it is unpredictably individual and local; in its public aspect, it is increasingly international and global. I now live in London, where so much of the world meets, and from where so much of it is accessible. This is a great enlargement of one's subjective world, and a great challenge: how to translate public awareness into private knowledge – for privacy is most necessary for the imagination to do its work – is, I find, the increasingly intricate, difficult and fascinating task.

Ogaga Ifowodo

The Writer's Many Worlds and the Task of Reconciliation

I have chosen the plural form, 'worlds' rather than the singular 'world', which might seem more apropos of an individual writer's reflection on his particular enabling time and place, or location, for more reasons than the suggestive theme of this volume, 'New Writing Worlds'. As W.E.B. Du Bois famously declared over a century ago, 'a double consciousness' defines the condition of the Negro, and by extension, the African. Brought on by the encounter between Europe and the rest of the world, the highly fraught history of that meeting has ensured that, as an African writer, I am condemned to inhabit two worlds simultaneously, and have constantly warring in me 'two unreconciled strivings two warring ideals.'

Du Bois's poignant words have spurred generations of writers and scholars to think of interpreting this consciousness as more than double, and to reconcile, as it were, the many warring worlds brought into the belly of the Ahabian whale. The most obvious spouting – to borrow some more from Melville – sign of the necessary doubleness of my writing world and vision is the language in which I write: English, the language of colonialism and a continuing neo-colonialism; a language whose world dominance today owes to the very history I have already evoked.

Yet, the writer, even as a cultural historian, is first and foremost, a human being – which is how come (s)he is a writer anyway! And if Wole Soyinka is right in his assertion that 'Justice is the first condition of humanity,' then the writer's 'world' must, inevitably, be double, nay, plural, encompassing other worlds. For even without recourse to Hegel's negative Master-Slave dialectic of subjectification and freedom, it is obvious that the same primal needs govern the deepest and shallowest urges of all human beings wherever collected on the earth. And that all themes, great and small, have been expounded upon in oral and written literatures from immemorial antiquity to the over-voluble now. Thus, Shakespeare might have addressed all but 28 of the sonnets to the singular male object of his irrepressible love, yet in Sonnet 76, he agonizes over the un-originality of the form and content of his poems, concluding thus:

O, know, sweet love, I always write of you,
And you and love are still my argument;
So all my best is dressing old words new,
Spending again what is already spent;
For as the sun is daily new and old,
So is my love, still telling what is told.

If love, whether as Eros or Agape – or for that matter, as the love
of money (said to be the root of all evil) and power – is what drives the
world, then writing of my native Nigeria out of love of the motherland
is at the same time no more than dressing all the worlds, without which
its existence is meaningless, in new words; all in the hope of effecting a
reconciliation of the Du Bosian debacle with which I began.

Kapka Kassabova *A Perverse Condition*

At a poetry festival in a small English town, I met a Venezuelan writer
living in Vienna.

'Are you crazy?' he said, 'You left Bulgaria, you came to live in
Britain, then you went to New Zealand, and now you come back to
Britain? Are you addicted to being an immigrant or what?'

'Well, look at yourself,' I said. He had previously lived in Mexico,
Argentina and Colombia. He didn't particularly love Vienna, and
couldn't even tell me why he was living there now.

'I know,' he said wistfully, 'I'm perverse.'

An immigrant is someone who arrives in a new place to rebuild her
home there. An exile is someone who was forcibly displaced. A traveller
is someone who seeks displacement. It is the space in between that I
inhabit, both in life and in literature, a paradoxical space of restlessness
and longing for the perfect home, perhaps a particular kind of 'perversion'
that rejects simplicity in favour of complexity and complication.

In a way, all writing takes place in that borderless virtual country
called Language which opens up among the many homelands we lose
in a lifetime: the past, people and places we love, even parts of ourselves.
Writing is an act of resistance against the erosion of our personal and
collective world by the forces of time. In that sense, writers tend to
spend a lot of time in that country regardless of their cultural

circumstances. But a literal sense of cultural 'in-betweenness' complements the writer's condition.

Without this 'in-betweenness', I would have never found myself – a Bulgarian New Zealander with a degree in French – reading my poetry in Spanish translation, with an Argentine accent acquired during my sojourns in Buenos Aires, at a Latin American festival in Vienna, organized by the same Venezuelan writer. These are the moments when the 'perversion' of a complicated identity can become a pleasure.

Anni Sumari

I regard myself as a poet (published six poetry collections so far), though I've written some lyrical prose as well. Here, I'd like to emphasize three aspects of my writing worlds.

I have one very clear aesthetic literary value, the one that's inspired me for years and years already. It's the all-devouring nature of poetry among the literary genres or senses. I feel that there is no word, no sentence, no idea, not a linguistic particular that could not become a part of a poem. It's the existing link between the un-verbal and verbal. In poetry, the everyday life and transcendental visions can merge. (I often like to build my poems like dramas, with dialogue and development, different voices coming from an unexpected direction interrupting the main voice or voices).

I am somewhat rootless, very individual, an outsider. I have family roots in at least four European countries. Born in a capital city, I lived in the countryside with my parents until I was 18, then returned to the capital as an urban girl. I protected that identity from other influences for 13 years – and have consequently been an outsider in all those rural villages in which I lived. I've travelled a lot; I love being on the road. Every poem in *The Years above the Waters* (2003) was written outside Finland, and named by the place where it was written. I don't feel I really have a home town or even a home country, though language is my fate, since I have only one native language, and my personal style is complicated enough to be satisfyingly expressed only in that language.

From the moment I first grabbed the books, until the age of 18 when I started to study literature, I read almost only translated literature. I cannot be associated with any Finnish literary tradition, trend or individual writer. (If I have any literary background, it is in European surrealism and French prose poetry). That's why they used to call me 'a cult poet' when I was younger. Now they only call me 'the violent poet' (!)

I think rootlessness is a good vaccine against unhealthy nationalism, racism and so on – when you feel that there is nothing you could call 'we, our values', then there is neither 'them, their values'.

George Szirtes *Veil and Soil*

Born in Budapest to a Hungarian Transylvanian mother and a Hungarian father of Moravian and Bohemian background, I married an English girl who had spent her childhood in Malaysia but was born in China to a Scottish mother. My brother's first marriage was to a half-Italian, half-Jamaican, and his second to the daughter of a Polish father. We are a mixed bunch.

Worlds seen like this are more veil than soil, and there is a kind of semi-transparency to them, so that the faces behind flutter a little and are not quite defined. But then neither is the viewer. T.S. Eliot warned of 'rootless cosmopolitans', by which he meant primarily Jews, but then he was an American, educated in France and living in London. *The Wasteland* is nothing if not veils and visions. But there is soil-world too, and it continues singing under our feet. I am a poet of the English language and partly of the English soil, but beneath it lies a veil of Hungarian soil out of which I translate. Veil over veil: soil on soil. The trick is to listen to the complex song such layering makes and try to render it up as best we can.

Luisa Valenzuela *New Writing Worlds*

I was asked to put down a few words about my writing worlds, and I am not too comfortable with the possessive though I am very happy with the plural. The writing worlds are not necessarily mine, but they are many, and they run across me when I'm lucky enough to access their geography. Worlds, words – similar doors for a writer who would like to push the boundaries. We have another challenge here: the word New. *New Writing Worlds* is the general title of our conversations, and I would love to contribute with new and different texts, that is to say, explore new territories. A pretension that can be often paralysing. A mini-nightmare I had some time ago can give a sense of what I'm trying to say:

I was in a car with some people on a dull stretch of highway. We were going pretty fast on our way to an unknown place. So unfamiliar that all the highway signs and markers and the street names disappeared as we got closer, leaving us only blank signs.

It was the night before flying to Mali, but I'm sure my dream was not factual. It had to do more with fiction writing, which I have been procrastinating over for quite a while – in search of a new approach, I tell myself as an excuse. Though perhaps in Mali I found a kind of answer: build beauty with mud, respecting the masks.

Mart Valjataga

I am a writer of formal verse and verbal games who often needs a technical challenge to trigger the creative impulse. These challenges may be related to formal linguistic puzzles, and they function as inspirational aids. Sometimes the final product is so far removed from the initial challenge that the latter is not perceivable in the former. Experimenting with formal verse, translating poetry, writing parodies or committed and occasional verse – these are the activities in which I feel most at home. It means setting quite an explicit task for oneself and trying to fulfil it as perfectly as possible. The formal constraints do not necessarily inhibit creative freedom, and the possibilities of language could manifest themselves even more vividly through strict rules. The unfortunate side of this kind of methodological approach, which has its affinities with the French Oulipo group, is that most of my verse remains untranslatable. The fortunate side is that these skills have enabled me to become a translator of poetry, and I hope I have been able to convey some essential qualities of great poets to my native language.

Mary Woronov   *Literary Value in Modern Time*

Writing exercises the imagination, which is starving in our modern world of super entertainment and invasive advertizing. The boredom of childhood is where I first learned to pretend. Later, the idea of stepping outside of reality to create an imaginary world with words was my escape. Once written down these words are no longer a part of me. Carrying their tools, maps, symbols and triggers, they enter the reader's mind. They find his imagination hiding from the drone of a TV somewhere, and unpacking their tools they make it perform, construct, picture, and feel again.

Example – knowing the usual facts, numbers, and propaganda about South Africa, I still felt less human for not being able to imagine what it's like for a country to change, and for not feeling the sympathy South Africans deserved. Reading *Disgrace* by J. M. Coetzee, I came away with an honest expression of grief, fear, and compassion for this country.

The imagination is a dying animal, dying from lack of exercise, suppressed by movies, which do all the work for you, betrayed when art traded its mysteries for concepts and ideas, and starving for more of poetry's metaphors. But fiction still uses old tools like emotion and narration to make our imaginations trot around the room again and even go outside in search of meaning.

Vesna Goldsworthy
The Trouble with Belonging: An Afterword

In late October 2005, I was invited to open the annual Book Fair in Belgrade. This is an event which encapsulates many of the similarities and differences between Serbia, where I was born, and Britain, where I now live. The opening of the Book Fair is a high point in the Serbian cultural season. It is a carefully staged event, broadcast live on the main TV channel, picked up as headline news in evening bulletins, and reported by a formidable host of print media.

Yes, some Serbs are passionate readers, but, even as a percentage of the overall population, they are probably not more numerous than their counterparts in Britain. Local bestseller lists are not that different from British ones. The foreign names that dominate them – J.K. Rowling, Dan Brown – would be familiar to any British reader. But perhaps one difference between the two countries is that even those Serbs who do not read much seem to believe that books – and writers – matter. Their perceived social importance is greater than in Britain, even if their advances and royalties are immeasurably smaller.

This respect for writers is not, I hasten to add, an undivided good. Anyone who has sat through an interminable interview on prime time television with the Serbian *écrivain du jour* pontificating on politics, government or the educational system – and without the kind of interruptions which are meted out to politicians – would bear this out. As Mart Valjataga says of the Estonian literary scene earlier in this volume, in small countries the writing of novels is impelled more by vanity than greed.

As a celebration of publishing, the Belgrade Book Fair has no parallel in Britain. The London Book Fair is much bigger both in terms of the business transacted and the sheer numbers of books on display, and much less significant. The crowds at the Belgrade events, including school children bussed in from all over the country to catch a glimpse of the writers whose names they know from their reading lists, are unimaginable in London where the Fair is mainly an exercise in business-to-business communication.

As a way of demonstrating one's love of books, as well as one's love of publicity, the opening ceremony is normally attended by Belgrade's elite: political party leaders, diplomats, prelates of the Orthodox church, and members of the Yugoslav royal family, now returned from their British exile, as well as, less surprisingly, academicians, university professors, and others who describe themselves as intellectuals (public and otherwise). *Le tout Serbie* turns up. On occasions such as these, and in small countries such as the one I come from, the imagined community that is the nation feels all too palpably real.

The country which nurtured me is one in which no one respects politicians, but most people respect most writers. However, I often have an impression that in Great Britain many more people dream of becoming writers. This is, perhaps, a function of a wealthier society, with its scores of creative writing classes and groups trading on the premium we place upon self-fulfilment, its countless festivals and other places of literary pilgrimage, and its fairy tales of multi-millionaire authors. I am not sure if this is still true, but a couple of years ago I was told that there was only one full-time writer in the whole of Serbia, yet there are days when it seems that most Londoners are writing a novel and I feel able to own up to it only in inverted commas: 'I', dear reader, am 'writing' a 'novel' too.

I was invited to Belgrade as a memoir writer. *Chernobyl Strawberries*, the story of my life that I originally wrote in English after 20 years of living – and what seemed like some months of dying – in Britain, was published in my native Serbian last October. It was somebody else's translation. Rather neurotically, I worried that, if I were to have undertaken the task of rendering it into Serbian, I couldn't stop myself from writing a completely different book.

* * *

Each year, a foreign country is invited to be the guest of honour at the Belgrade Book Fair, and its writers attract special attention. In 2005, which was also the golden jubilee of the Fair, it was the United Kingdom's turn. I was invited not as a local author (that honour belonged to a white-haired academician with strong views on the disappearance of the Cyrillic alphabet), but as a British writer. Although I may be audibly different from other British authors, I am also, paradoxically, a 'typical' face on the British literary scene, where being of foreign 'extraction' (I love the word!) barely seems worth registering any more.

In Belgrade, the exact composition of the British team was guessed at for weeks beforehand. Might it be Ian McEwan, Zadie Smith, Julian Barnes or even Salman Rushdie? Would the British Council be able to entice any literary 'giants' to a country which, while it may worship books, also represents a tiny market, where anything over a 1,000 copies sold is a bestseller and advances are such that British agents would barely be able to afford a sandwich out of their cut? It is also a country that is struggling to supplant memories of the 1990s and its role in the wars of the Yugoslav succession with something more positive, although I am not sure whether this would be a point of interest or a deterrent.

Obviously, I am no Zadie Smith, and my literary star shines only for those with stronger telescopes. I was booked for readings and signings relatively early on, but not for the opening ceremony or, rather, not until I emerged as the last minute compromise candidate. Away from the public eye, and unbeknown to me, the question of who exactly was to be the British representative at the opening ceremony was causing a degree of *froideur* between the host nation and the guest of honour. What was at stake reflects an important difference in the literary wavelengths upon which my two countries operate.

I am not sure how exactly the negotiations unfolded. Apparently, a week or so before the event, the British side put forward the name of a popular British writer whose sales figures muster more noughts on the end than I can hope for. The choice made sense in every way but one. The distinction between popular literature and 'high' literature (or, simply, 'Literature') is much clearer in Belgrade than it is in the UK, where decades of chipping away at the canon have made it more difficult to be certain that there is some essential difference between Jilly Cooper and Ian McEwan. In the UK, as Amit Chaudhuri observes in this volume, only agents and publishers continue to talk about 'master-pieces', and 'essential reading' implies the exact opposite. In Belgrade, the so-called popular writer, however good he or she may be, is definitely not the sort of writer who is supposed to cut ribbons at august book events. I am not sure that any of this mattered much for the writer concerned. Excluded from the opening ceremony, he had an excellent time in Serbia signing books for crowds of excited fans and explaining ideas of marriage and fatherhood to delighted interviewers on Belgrade television.

I was 'appointed' (or 'anointed'?) literally at the eleventh hour; late enough to have to fly to Belgrade via Munich on a small plane full of German businessmen in order to make it on time for the sound tests. I found the occasion fascinating. In fact, as someone who taught English Literature and wrote about it for many years before trying to contribute to it, I found the local media response to my role almost more interesting than the event itself. My champions, I am glad to say, were considerably more numerous than my detractors, but the latter had some interesting arguments. Whom should I have really represented: Britain or Serbia? Am I a British writer of Serbian origin or a Serbian writer? I delivered my speech in English, as I was asked to do; should I or should I not have accepted? Finally, a tabloid columnist asked whether someone who has not written a novel should have been accorded the great honour. (Yes, the tabloids are somewhat different over there). However literary my style may be, memoir was obviously suspect as a genre. It belonged not in the field of belles lettres but somewhere between art and craft, I guess. Without a novel, I am, it seems, only halfway there. 'Until you show us you can do it, sister, there is nothing to discuss', the columnist challenged me, in an aside.

* * *

In the press conferences and interviews that followed the opening, I had to give quick, two-line answers to complex questions about my own writing. I found the Norwich exchanges gathered in this book particularly useful in thinking about what I was asked. Did I exoticize the world of my childhood for my English readers or did I emphasize its similarities with the West? What are the implications of writing in English for my sense of belonging? Is my Serbian past embedded in my mother tongue in a way which makes my work akin to translation, with Serbian as the shadowy signifier in every English transaction I make? What do I, having written a literary memoir, feel about the hierarchy of genres in which the novel seems so often to be the undisputed king?

I am not sure my answers were particularly profound. However, I found myself, again and again, remembering the New Writing Worlds Symposium and the discussions in which 40 writers took part. These were precisely the sorts of questions we tried to address and the sorts of experiences we exchanged in the course of the four days, when we met for a couple of hours in the morning and a couple of hours in the afternoon, dispersed for workshops with writing groups in Norwich and gathered again for evening readings of poetry and fiction on the University of East Anglia campus. It gradually became clear to me that something important had taken shape amid these exchanges, and that, although coming from very different places, we had achieved consensus on a number of the questions I faced in Belgrade.

I accepted the offer to edit the essays and transcripts of conversations collected in this volume in order to put that impression to the test. What is gathered here, in addition to specially commissioned reflections on some of the topics with which we were dealing, represents the formal, taped portion of our conversations, and it reflects the themes – of the moral and political duty of literature, of language and belonging, place and displacement – which seemed to preoccupy us most.

Many of the events during those four days were open to the public. I remember, for example, Leila Ahmed, Dubravka Ugresic and Eva Hoffman discussing the nature of memory, and Graham Swift reading from *The Light of Day* in a way that made reading as exciting as the best theatre. Unlike most writing festivals where one catches glimpses of fellow writers in the Green Room, here writers formed part of each other's audience, and the experience in turn enriched our daily conversations. The symposium itself took place in a series of meetings behind the (semi-)closed doors of the Council Room at the University of East Anglia. The room was, many of us observed, not dissimilar to the Security Council at the United Nations, both in the clean and grand modernist lines of Denys Lasdun's architectural design and in terms of its multi-lingual, multi-ethnic and multi-generational occupants.

Norwich was in the throes of a heatwave. The landscaped grounds of the UEA campus reminded me of Teletubby-land, with dozens of fat tame rabbits moving very slowly across the well-tended lawns, seemingly oblivious to passers-by. They seemed so happy on campus that I jested they must be my fellow academics, reincarnated. It all formed a somewhat surreal background for our conversations which, whatever the ostensible starting point, kept returning to what I see as the 'big' questions of writing, the kinds of questions which, however important, are so rarely tackled in the academic conferences to which I am used.

They included topics such as: what is literary value and can it be usefully defined? Do we have a duty towards the past as keepers of memory or are we free to sculpt it and remodel it as we like? Should we worry about globalization or embrace the new opportunities it offers? Are we witnessing the end of national literatures and the beginning of world literature? Is the novel, about whose death we seem to fret at regular intervals, in fact the tyrant-genre, the giant rhododendron under whose shadows nothing much is allowed to grow?

Many of those attempting to answer such questions on these pages are teachers, publishers and translators of literature, as well as writers. The conversations and essays included in this book are informed by literary theory, but they are also, and in the best possible way, post-theoretical. They do not avoid important political questions but nor do they circle obsessively around the politics of the day. They mirror a variety of the challenges writers face in different countries but they also reflect many of the reasons why, as someone said in one of our conversations, writing is still quite possibly the best job that there is.

Who's Who

Leila Ahmed

Egyptian-US memoirist, critic and academic Leila Ahmed was appointed to the Women's Studies in Religion professorship at Harvard Divinity School in 1999, the first woman to occupy that chair. She was previously Professor of Women's Studies and Near Eastern Studies at the University of Massachusetts. Professor Ahmed's latest book is the widely acclaimed memoir *A Border Passage*. Other publications include *Women and Gender in Islam: The Historical Roots of a Modern Debate*.

Lisa Appignanesi

Lisa Appignanesi was born in Poland and grew up in Paris and Montreal, before moving to Britain. With a PhD in comparative literature, she was a university lecturer before becoming Deputy Director of London's Institute of Contemporary Arts. She is the bestselling author of eight novels, including most recently, *The Memory Man* (Arcadia) and *Sanctuary* (Bantam), as well as of various works of non-fiction. She is also a noted broadcaster, critic and cultural commentator, the Deputy President of English PEN, and a Chevalier des Arts et des Lettres.

Mourid Barghouti

Mourid Barghouti was born on the West Bank near Ramallah in 1944. He has published 13 books of poetry in Arabic including *Collected Works* (1997), and was awarded the Palestine Award for Poetry in 2000. His latest book *I Saw Ramallah*, an account of his return to Palestine after 30 years in exile in Cairo, was published in English by Bloomsbury (2004) to great critical acclaim. Mourid Barghouti lives in Cairo with his wife, the novelist Radwa Ashour.

Gillian Beer

Dame Gillian Beer was recently King Edward VII Professor of English Literature at the University of Cambridge and is a Fellow of the British

Academy. Her books include *Darwin's Plots, Open Fields: Science in Cultural Encounter* and *Virginia Woolf: The Common Ground*. She was Chair of the Poetry Book Society for four years, and has twice been a judge for the Booker Prize, as well as the Orange Prize and the David Cohen Prize for Literature.

Christopher Bigsby

Christopher Bigsby is Professor of American Studies at the University of East Anglia. He has published more than 30 books on aspects of English and American culture, from African-American literature and popular culture to theatre. He is also joint editor (with Don Wilmeth at Brown University) of *The Cambridge History of the American Theatre (3 vols)*. In 2000 and 2001, he also published two volumes of his interviews with writers. He is the author of four novels: *Hester, Pearl, Still Lives* and *Beautiful Dreamer,* and has written for radio and television. He is a regular broadcaster and organizer of an annual International Literary Festival and he is Director of The Arthur Miller Centre.

Ron Butlin

Ron Butlin was born in Edinburgh. His poetry and fiction have won several Scottish Arts Council Book Awards and a Poetry Book Society Recommendation. The French translation of his novel *The Sound of My Voice* was awarded Le Prix Mille Pages 2004 for Best Foreign Novel and Le Prix Lucioles 2005 for Best Foreign Novel. A 'regular' at the Edinburgh International Book Festival, he has participated in many major literary festivals in Britain and abroad.

Amit Chaudhuri

Amit Chaudhuri was born in Calcutta in 1962, and grew up in Bombay. He gained his DPhil at Oxford University. His novels include: *A Strange and Sublime Address* (1991, winner of first prize in The Betty Trask Awards for a first novel, and the Commonwealth Writers' Prize for Best First Book, Eurasia), *Afternoon Raag* (1993, the Society of Authors' Encore Prize and the Southern Arts Literature Prize), and

Freedom Song (1998). His fourth novel, *A New World*, won the Sahitya Akademi award 2002, India's highest literary honour for a single book. Amit has held many creative and academic posts, and has written for most of the world's major journals. His book of short stories, *Real Time*, was published in 2002.

Austin Clarke

Austin Clarke was born in Barbados in 1934 and emigrated to Canada to attend the University of Toronto. He won the 1999 W.O. Mitchell Prize, and has published numerous novels and short story collections, including *The Polished Hoe*, winner of the Commonwealth Prize for best book 2003. Austin Clarke was a leader of the civil rights movement in Toronto in the 60s and 70s, and assisted in setting up the Black Studies programmes at Yale and Harvard. He has served as Visiting Professor at many leading American universities, and held posts including cultural attaché of the Barbardian Embassy in Washington and advisor to the Prime Minister of Barbados.

David Constantine

David Constantine was born in Salford, 1944, and was Fellow in German at Queen's College, Oxford, until 2000. His poetry includes *Watching for Dolphins* (1983, winner of the Alice Hunt Bartlett Award), *Something for the Ghosts* (2002, shortlisted for the Whitbread Prize), and *Collected Poems* (2004). Translations include Friedrich Hölderlin's *Selected Poems* (European Poetry Translation prize, 1997), and Goethe's *Faust* (Penguin, 2005). He has also published the novel *Davies*, the short story collection *Under the Dam* (Comma Press, 2005), and the biography *Sir William Hamilton, Fields of Fire* (2001). He is a co-editor of *Modern Poetry in Translation*.

Jon Cook

Jon Cook is Professor of Literature, Dean of the Faculty of Arts and Humanities and Director of the Centre for Creative and Performing Arts at the University of East Anglia. The Centre hosts the Spring

International Literary Festival at UEA and the Visiting Writers series at the Savile Club in London. He was convenor of the MA in Creative Writing at UEA from 1986-1996. His most recent book is *Poetry in Theory* (2004). His next book, *Hazlitt in Love*, will be published in 2007.

Alison Croggon

Alison Croggon writes poetry, prose, criticism and theatre texts. Her poetry includes *This is the Stone*, (Penguin Books Australia), *The Blue Gate* (Black Pepper Press) and *Mnemosyne* (Wild Honey Press). Awards include the Anne Elder and Dame Mary Gilmore Prizes. *Attempts at Being* was published by Salt in 2002 and *The Common Flesh: New and Selected Poems* by Arc Publications UK in 2003. Her young adult fantasy novels, the *Pellinor* series, are published by Walker Books in the UK, and her theatre texts have been widely produced in Australia.

Tessa de Loo

Dutch novelist Tessa de Loo is the author of the bestselling novel *The Twins*, which sold over three million copies, and was made into the Oscar nominated film, *Twin Sisters* – the most widely-viewed film in Dutch cinema history. Her other prize-winning novels include *A Bed In Heaven, Meander, Isabelle, The Smoke Sacrifice* and *The Miracle of the Dog*, while *A Pig in the Palace* looks at Byron's travels in Albania. *The Twins* was chosen as one of the *Sunday Times* '100 Best Books of the Year'. Tessa de Loo now lives in Portugal.

Bernardine Evaristo

Bernardine Evaristo's novel *Soul Tourists* (Penguin 2005) is a modern-day car journey across Europe featuring ghosts of colour from European history. She is also the author of two critically acclaimed novels-in-verse: *The Emperor's Babe* (Penguin, 2001), and *Lara* (ARP 1997). She frequently tours abroad and has been writer-in-residence or visiting professor at many leading universities. She became a Fellow of the Royal Society of Literature in 2004, and won a NESTA Fellowship Award in 2003.

Moris Farhi

Born in Ankara, Turkey, in 1935, Moris Farhi is the author of five novels, including *Young Turk*, (Saqi, March, 2004), which was shortlisted for the Wingate Prize 2005, and *Children of the Rainbow*, winner of the Amico Rom prize 2002 and the Special prize from the Roma Academy of Culture and Sciences in Germany, 2003. He is a widely published poet, and a Vice President of International PEN. Moris Farhi was appointed an MBE for services to literature in 2001, and is a Fellow of both the Royal Society of Literature and the Royal Geographical Society.

Vesna Goldsworthy

Vesna Goldsworthy was born in Belgrade in 1961, and was already an acclaimed poet and successful radio presenter by the time she left Yugoslavia in 1986. Since arriving in England, she has worked in publishing, for the BBC World Service, and as a university teacher. Her first book, *Inventing Ruritania: The Imperialism of the Imagination* (Yale 1998) was translated into four languages. Her second, a best-selling memoir entitled *Chernobyl Strawberries*, was published by Atlantic in 2005 to broad critical acclaim, and translated into German and Serbian. It was serialized in *The Times* and read by Vesna herself as *Book of the Week* on Radio Four.

Xiaolu Guo

Xiaolu Guo was born in a fishing village in south China in 1973. She was awarded an MA in Film from the Beijing Film Academy in 2000 and has worked as a novelist, essayist, screenwriter and filmmaker. Her first novel *Village of Stone* was published by Chatto, and shortlisted for the 2005 Independent Foreign Fiction Prize. Having studied documentary film at the National Film and Television School in London, she now lives in London.

Helon Habila

Helon Habila was born in 1967. He worked as a lecturer and a journalist in Nigeria, and was the African Writing Fellow at the University of East Anglia from 2002-2004. His first novel, *Waiting for an Angel* (Penguin, 2003) won the Commonwealth Writers' Prize for Best First Book (Africa Region). It tells the story of Lomba, a young journalist living in Lagos under Nigeria's brutal regime. Helon Habila was also a winner of the Caine Prize, 2001. His novel *Measuring Time* will be published in 2006.

Choman Hardi

Choman Hardi was born in Iraqi Kurdistan. Having spent the early period of her childhood as a refugee in Iran, Choman Hardi and her family were forced to flee there again when the Iraqi government used chemical weapons on the Kurds in 1988. She came to England in 1993, and studied at Queen's College, Oxford. Choman Hardi has published three collections of poetry in Kurdish, as well as the collection *Life for us* in English (Bloodaxe, 2004.) She was chair of the Exiled Writers Ink! from 2001-2003, and was recently awarded a PhD for her work on the mental health of Kurdish women.

Eva Hoffman

Eva Hoffman grew up in Cracow, Poland. After emigrating to Canada in her teens, she studied in the US and received her PhD from Harvard University. She has worked as senior editor and writer for *The New York Times* and is the author of one novel, *The Secret*, and four works of non-fiction, including *Lost in Translation: A Life in a New Language* and *After Such Knowledge: Memory, History and the Legacy of the Holocaust*. She has received a Guggenheim Fellowship, a prize from the American Academy of Arts and Letters, a Whiting Award for Writing and the Prix Italia for radio.

Aamer Hussein

Aamer Hussein was born in Karachi, Pakistan, in 1955. He came to Britain in 1970 and graduated from SOAS, going on to teach Urdu at its Language Centre for many years. He is the author of the acclaimed short story collections: *Mirror to the Sun* (1993), *This Other Salt* (1999), *Turquoise* (2003), and *Cactus Town: Selected Stories* (2003). Also a literary critic and translator, he has rediscovered several forgotten Urdu classics, particularly by women. He is a Fellow of the Royal Society of Literature.

Ogaga Ifowodo

Ogaga Ifowodo was born in 1966 in Oleh, Delta State, Nigeria. A lawyer, he holds an MFA from Cornell University. He has published *Homeland & Other Poems* (1998), winner of the Association of Nigerian Authors poetry prize; *Madiba*, winner of the 2003 ANA/Cadbury poetry prize; *The Oil Lamp* (2005); and *Homeland* (1999.) He worked for eight years with the Civil Liberties Organization, Nigeria's premier human rights group, and from 1997-1998 was held under preventive detention by the then military regime of General Sani Abacha on account of his human rights activism. He is currently pursuing a PhD in English and Cultural Studies at Cornell University.

Kapka Kassabova

Kapka Kassabova, born in 1973, is a poet, novelist and travel writer. Bulgarian-born and bred, she was educated in Bulgaria, Britain, and New Zealand. Her first book of poetry *All Roads Lead to the Sea* (Auckland University Press 1997) won a NZ Montana Book Award for best first poetry book. The first of her two novels, *Reconnaissance* (Penguin NZ), won the 2000 Commonwealth Writers' Prize for best first novel, South-East Asia-Pacific Region. Her latest poetry collection is *Someone Else's Life* (2003, Bloodaxe/Auckland University Press).

Hasso Krull

Hasso Krull, born in 1964, is a well-known cultural figure in Estonia. As a popular teacher and shaper of social thought, he has succeeded in familiarizing Estonian readers with European thinkers such as Jacques Derrida and Michel Foucault. Krull is primarily known, however, as a poet, most notably with the collection *Poems 1987-1991* (Luuletused 1987-1991, published in 1993.) Krull also writes on history, politics, art, film and philosophy, and contributes to the periodical *Ninnik*, which focuses on poetry in translation.

Rattawut Lapcharoensap

Rattawut Lapcharoensap was born in Chicago and raised in Bangkok. Educated at Triamudomsuksa Pattanakan and Cornell University, he went on to receive an MFA in Creative Writing from the University of Michigan. His highly acclaimed volume of short stories, *Sightseeing*, was shortlisted for the *Guardian* First Book Award 2005. He has also been David T.K. Wong Fellow at the University of East Anglia.

Ib Michael

Danish writer Ib Michael, born in 1945, has written poems, travel books, short stories and, first and foremost, novels, which have garnered him a huge audience both in Denmark and abroad. His novel *Prince* was published in English in 2001 to great critical acclaim, and his latest book *Grill* is a highly topical literary thriller about war, love and ethnic troubles (Glydendal 2005).

Ignacio Padilla

Ignacio Padilla, born in 1968, was raised in Mexico City. After researching a PhD on Cervantes in Salamanca, Spain, his debut novel, *La catedral de los ahogados*, won Mexico's Juan Rulfo prize for a new author. In 1996, Padilla and a group of colleagues launched the manifesto of the 'Crack' group, which aims to renew Mexican fiction. His novel, *Amphitryon*, won the 2000 Premio Primavera in Spain, and was published in English by Scribner as *Shadow without a Name*. Padilla was also Mexico's cultural attaché in London in 2000.

David Solway

David Solway has written many books of poetry including the award-winning *Modern Marriage; Bedrock; Chess Pieces; Saracen Island;* and *Franklin's Passage,* winner of Le Grand Prix du Livre de Montréal. Prose publications include *Education Los*, which won the QSPELL Prize for Non-Fiction, and *Random Walks*, a finalist for Le Grand Prix du Livre de Montréal. Solway publishes regularly in journals and magazines, and his poetry has been widely anthologized. A new collection of poems, *The Pallikari of Nesmine Rifat*, was released by Goose Lane Editions in 2005.

Anni Sumari

Anni Sumari was born in Helsinki, Finland, in 1965. She has published 10 books, mostly of poetry, as well as a travelogue about a writers' train that toured Europe in 2000 (*Train Play, 2001*). She studied general literature and media/communication studies at the University of Helsinki (Master of Arts 1991). Her translations into Finnish include works by Samuel Beckett, Robert Antoni and Bernardine Evaristo. She has also retold a selection of Scandinavian myths, to be published in 2007, and edited several anthologies of Finnish and Nordic poetry for international book markets. Sumari was awarded The Dancing Bear Price (founded by the Finnish National Broadcasting Co.) for the best poetry book of 1998 for her collection *Measure and Degree*. Her poems have been translated into 18 languages.

Graham Swift

Graham Swift was born in London in 1949. He is the author of seven novels, including *Waterland*, which was shortlisted for the Booker Prize and won the *Guardian* Fiction Award, the Winifred Holtby Memorial Prize and the Italian Premio Grinzane Cavour; *Ever After*, which won the French Prix du Meilleur Livre Étranger; and *Last Orders*, which won the 1996 Booker Prize. He has also published a collection of short stories, *Learning to Swim*. His most recent novel is *The Light of Day*.

George Szirtes

Born in Budapest in 1948, poet and artist George Szirtes came to England as a refugee, following the Hungarian Uprising in 1956, and trained as a painter in Leeds and London. He became a Fellow of the Royal Society of Literature in 1982, and has since won many awards for his work; his latest poetry collection, *Reel* (2004) won the T. S. Eliot Prize. George Szirtes teaches Creative Writing at the Norwich School of Art and Design and the University of East Anglia.

Dubravka Ugresic

Dubravka Ugresic was born in the former Yugoslavia (Croatia), and is presently based in Amsterdam. She writes novels, short stories and essays, and her books have been translated into many European languages. She has received several prestigious international literary awards, including the Charles Veillon European Essay for *The Culture of Lies* in 1996. Ugresic is also a literary scholar and occasionally teaches, mostly at the American universities.

Luisa Valenzuela

Luisa Valenzuela was born in Buenos Aires. In 1979 she moved to New York, where she has been a fellow of the New York Institute for the Humanities since 1982. She has been a Guggenheim Fellow, a Fullbright Fellow, and is also a graduate of the International Writers' Program, Iowa. English translations of her books include the short story collections *Open Door, The Censors* and *Symmetries,* and the novels *Clara, He Who Searches, The Lizard's Tail* and *Bedside Manners.*

Mart Valjataga

Poet, translator and editor Mart Valjataga was born in 1965, and lives in Tallinn. He studied linguistics at the University of Tartu, underwent military service in the Soviet army, and then studied at Indiana University. Since 1987, he has edited the cultural journal *Vikerkaar*, for the last decade as Editor-in-Chief. Besides poetry translations, criticism, reviews and journalism, he has published two poetry books, the most recent being *Sada tuhat miljardit millenniumisonetti /100 000 000 000 000 millennial poems.*

Philippe Vasset

French novelist Philippe Vasset edits the investigative newsletter *Africa Energy Intelligence*, based in Paris. He worked as a corporate detective in the US before becoming a journalist and, in 1993, won the prize of Best Young Writer awarded by the French daily *Le Monde*. Following his debut *ScriptGenerator©®™*, he has since written a second novel.

Mary Woronov

US writer, film actress, director and artist Mary Woronov began her career in New York with the Theater of the Ridiculous, and has starred in many films including Andy Warhol's *Chelsea Girls* and *Screen Tests*, and Oliver Stone's *Seizure*. Her first love had always been painting – until she started writing at the age of 50. Her books include *Swimming Underground, My Years in the Warhol Factory* (2000), the novels *Snake* (2000) and *Niagara* (2002); and *Blind Love* (short stories, 2004.) All are published by Serpent's Tail.

A.B. Yehoshua

Born in Jerusalem, 1936, A. B. Yehoshua is the author of *The Lover, The Continuing Silence of a Poet, Mr Mani, Open Heart, A Journey to the End of the Millennium* and *The Liberated Bride*. He is one of Israel's pre-eminent novelists and has been awarded the prestigious Israel Prize for his lifetime's creative contribution to Israel, the National Jewish Book Award in the US and the Jewish Quarterly-Wingate Prize in the UK. A.B. Yehoshua was listed for the Man Booker International Prize in 2005.

THE NEW WRITING PARTNERSHIP

e New Writing Partnership is a unique enterprise, based in Norwich, that aims to highlight, develop and pport creative writing, establishing the East of England as a centre of excellence. We seek to explore as ationships between writers, culture and local communities and stimulate debate about writing and we will ow writing wherever it leads – to the screen, to the stage, into the classroom, into the pubs, on to the web, he streets, into the media and of course into books.

EW WRITING WORLDS

w Writing Worlds brings writers from around the world together to celebrate the act of writing, and to bate the nature of literature across cultures. At the heart of the programme is a symposium held at the rld-renowned centre for creative writing, the University of East Anglia, and a series of public events, dings and workshops in Norwich and Norfolk. The New Writing Worlds series was launched in 2005, en 40 writers from around the globe came to Norwich to discuss the concept of *Literary Value*. New iting Worlds 2006 will take the concept of *Experiment* as its primary theme. This series will culminate in nal international congress in 2009.

EW WRITING VENTURES

eries of national prizes and awards for previously unpublished writers is organized each year by The New iting Partnership in collaboration with Arts Council England, East and Booktrust. These awards are signed to help launch the careers of writers who are expected to make an impact on the world of books d readers in the coming years. Awards are made in three categories: fiction, poetry and literary non-tion. The winner in each category will receive £5,000; the winners and two shortlisted authors from each tegory will also receive a place on the year-long Ventures development programme, which includes dividual mentoring, workshops and professional presentation.

SCALATOR LITERATURE

part of Arts Council England, East's Escalator programme of development for artists in the region, The w Writing Partnership manages the selection of 10 talented writers in the East in order to support their rk over a period of 6-12 months through the Grants for the Arts scheme. In 2004 ten poets were selected, 2005 ten fiction writers, and in 2006 we will select from creative non-fiction writers, writers for children and ung people and fiction writers, under the heading of prose.

EW WRITING TYPES

w Writing Types is an annual gathering for emerging writers with a serious commitment to their craft and eative process. The Lab offers intensive development work through a series of workshops and seminars. lit into three strands, fiction, creative non-fiction and poetry, the Lab is for writers with a desire to explore eir imaginations and the rigours of their craft. We also offer writers the opportunity to meet professional ters, editors, critics and publishers at The Forum, a series of lively debates, panel discussions and adings which address the professional aspects of the writing life and the industry that both supports and rrounds it. New Writing Types is a unique event that seeks to inform and inspire new writers in the rsuance of their career.

r full details, register for updates at info@newwritingpartnership.org.uk or ee our website for regular updates at www.newwritingpartnership.org.uk

The British Centre for Literary Translation

Raising the profile of literary translation in the UK

Translation today is situated at the heart of literary writing, as the evidence in 'Writing Worlds 1: The Norwich Exchanges' shows.

BCLT has something to offer everyone with a love of literature and an enthusiasm for exploring new horizons.

Workshops
Readings
Seminars
Publications
Research
Translation Residencies

Join our free mailing list and receive a complimentary issue of our journal In Other Words.

British Centre for Literary Translation
School of Literature & Creative Writing
University of East Anglia
Norwich, Norfolk, NR4 7TJ, UK
bclt@uea.ac.uk   +44 (0)1603 592785

www. literarytranslation.com